Living
Out Loud
in a Silent World

A 40-Day
Devotional for
Youth

By

Miracle Reed

ISBN: 978-0-9904779-0-7 (paperback)

ISBN: 978-0-9904779-1-4 (eBook)

Introduction

In today's society there are many things competing for your attention, from social media to reality TV. However, there is one who not only wants your attention, but deserves your attention as well. The one we are talking about is Jesus Christ. He alone deserves your time, attention, focus, and devotion. According to John 3:16 God gave his one and only son, Jesus Christ, just for you. Not because we were perfect, but because he knew we would need him to be with us in our imperfection. What an amazing love God has. Despite everything we have done against Him, He welcomes us with opportunities to receive forgiveness and come back to Him!

The world is searching for truth and what they are searching for, you have. That's right! God has created you to be a light in a dark world. God desires to use you so that you may be a voice of hope in a silent world. In the days ahead you will be challenged to live, speak up, pray more, and become more intentional and deliberate in your pursuit of God. Daily, God is pursuing you and longing for your time. For the next 40 days, your journey with God will change your pursuit for Him.

You may have questions and even doubts about what God desires and what your purpose is. As you begin this 40 day journey of being bold and courageous, rest assured, you will gain clarity and understanding. Life is not limited to what you make of it, it is also what you allow and who you let in. Each day you have a decision to either represent the light, who is Christ, or represent darkness, who is the enemy (the devil). This may sound simple at first, but keep in mind how the enemy does appear as an "angel of light" and can be difficult to identify. Sometime he appears through friends, inappropriate TV shows, music videos, parties, etc. However, you have been given power to stand against temptation, peer pressure, and fear. According to 1 John 4:4, you are greater than he that is in the entire world.

I know, sometimes it can be challenging to know what to do or say when friends and even family do not agree with your love and decision to live for God. Be encouraged because God knew what your journey would look like and all of the problems that would come your way. He has created real solutions for you in His Word. For the next 40 days you will be challenged to study God's word; begin a journey of self-discovery; live confidently and free from the thoughts and opinions of peers; and to live life "Out Loud in a Silent World".

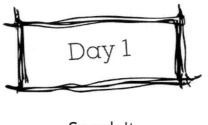

Day 1

Speak It

"In the beginning God created the heavens and the earth. The earth was formless and empty, and darkness covered the deep waters. And the spirit of the God was hovering over the surface of the waters. Then God said, 'Let there be light,' and there was light. And God saw that the light was good. Then he separated the light from the darkness. God called the light 'day' and the darkness 'night'." Genesis 1:1-3

In this life you have been given choices. These choices often help you see who you are when no one is looking and who you are while trying to meet the approval of others. According to Genesis, God created the day with three words, "let there be". This not only identifies the power God has but it also allows you to see that there are no limits to what God can do with his words. As a young person you have been given the chance to make a difference in this world with the words you speak as well. It doesn't matter how old you are, where you were born, or who your parents are. God has a plan for your life and from the beginning of time; God has been speaking life into existence.

In this 40 day journey you must ask yourself, "What have I been speaking into existence?" If God chose to speak life and everything we see, how much more has God made available to you? You have been called for this time to not only look around at the greatness of God in this magnificent world He created according to Genesis chapter one and two, but also find your place and purpose in this world. There are friends who will not agree with you and will not understand your decision to *live out loud.* You were not created to "fit in"; you have been created to stand "out."

As you read the first two chapters of Genesis, imagine what it must have been like to see the waters separate, vegetables come from the ground, and Eve being created from Adam's rib. Everything that took place in these chapters is a miraculous wonder of God. He created the entire world, not with his hands, but with his words. Wow! Do you realize that there in you is the power of God upon you accepting Him as your Lord and Savior? According to Proverbs 18:21, the tongue can bring death or life; those who love to talk will reap the consequences.

This means that you have the ability to speak words of power. This is no limited to the benefits you can receive but the ways in which you can bless others. Your decision to speak words of life, is your decision to choose to uplift a friend, talk a peer out of suicide and even present a reason to live That's right, your life is one of power and great influence. Speak It!

Scripture Readings

Genesis 1-2; Proverbs 18:21; Matthew 12:36

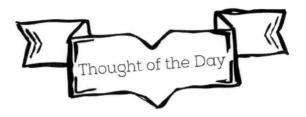

Thought of the Day

"The words that have been spoken are the reality of what is seen."

Questions: (for thought or discussion)

- If every word that you spoke was posted on a billboard, how would people describe you?
- If you could speak something into existence for your generation what would it be?
- Think of a time when you chose to speak life, as in Proverbs 18:21. How did it make you feel?

Today's Challenge

Offer a word of prayer with a friend.

Day 2

Just Do it

---

*"The Lord had said to Abram, 'Leave your
native country, your relatives, and your
father's family, and go to the land that I will
show. I will make you into a great nation. I will
bless you and make you famous, and you will
be a blessing to others. I will bless those who
bless you and curse those who treat you with
contemp. All the families on earth will be
blessed through you." Genesis 12:1-3*

Have you ever had to give up something you cared about a great deal? Maybe it was your favorite pet that had to be put to sleep; the opportunity to have your very first job; someone you were interested in dating; or even some of your friends who were negative influences. In having to give up what we value creates a void and sometimes uncertainty. You may not even know why you had to let go of some things or even some people. As you read "Living Out Loud" my prayer is for you to rediscover how God is working in and through our lives and in the decisions we make. Never forget, God is with you and he desires to fill every void.

Sometimes you may feel like Abram, like God is asking for you to leave behind everything familiar. You are right, that is exactly what God is doing. God is inviting you to a life without limits or familiarity. In this new way of life you are able to completely rely and depend on Him. It is a challenge to do this because we all have the natural desire to be in charge, which can create problems. However, when you are willing to let go of your plan and embrace God's plan, look at what He can do: Make you a great nation (ability to influence), Bless You (blow you away by what he does) and Make you famous (He will bring you before people as an inspiration).

Society has a way of painting a picture of the world willing to offer you riches and fame. But, when you turn on your television what do you see? Arrests, drug usage, suicide, murder, and misery? This is what we see daily in the media. It is dressed up with *Cribs, Reality TV, and lots of money.* According to Genesis 12 all Abram had to do was follow the instructions of God. He did not have to take his clothes off, he did not have to steal, cheat, or deceive. All he had to do was follow. Right now, in this very moment, God is calling you to follow him. Allow Him to fill those areas of emptiness left by everything you have let go to follow Christ. Just do it. Follow him.

Scripture Readings

Genesis 12; Matthew 16:24-26; John14:6

"*If currently all you had was a result of what God gave because of what you let go of, what would you have?*" *Life is not about what you can acquire but all that you give unto the glory of God*".

Questions: (for thought or discussion)

- What would you identify as being the biggest sacrifice you have made for God?
- Do you believe God will fill every area of your life? If so, in what ways do you think he will do it?
- Where are you currently, in relation to Matthew 16:24-26? Have you given your life or are you holding on to it?

Post an encouraging and inspirational post on social media (i.e., Twitter, Facebook or Instagram).

Day 3

Good World Gone Bad

"The Lord observed the extent of human wickedness on earth, and he saw that everything the thought or imagined was consistently and totally evil. So the Lord was sorry he had ever made them and put them on earth. It broke his heart." Genesis 6:5-6

You may be wandering how could God create the world and humans, say that "it is good" and then feel sorry that he made people. Your question is important so let's dive into what has taken place. In the beginning, when God created man and woman, they had no sin in their lives. However, in Genesis 3, Adam and Eve disobey the instructions given by God. They eat from the tree that God had said not to eat from. As result of their disobedience to God, their eyes were open to the *Knowledge of Good and Evil*, which ultimately led to them thinking independently from God.

Decisions we make can either lead to the path that has been created by God, or lead to the path that has been created by man. There is no doubt that any decision made outside of God's will ultimately leads to destruction and that is exactly what is being seen in this scripture. During your daily reading you will see that Noah had favor with God and also with his family. When God plans to floods the earth, Noah is given instructions to build a boat, "The Ark," as a means of protection and provision. Despite the mass destruction of the world, God presented a way of escape for Noah and those who were a part of his family. There may be situations going on in your life that cause you to feel forgotten because of the hurt you have experienced. But, be encouraged. You have not been left behind. Even at this moment God is presenting a way of escape for you.

In a world that has gone bad, God is raising you up as a generational leader to show the way. There are friends you spend time with daily and God is challenging you to be a light to them. Do not allow what your friends do to keep you from doing what God has called you to do. After the flood God made a promise that He would not destroy the earth because of the human race (Genesis 8:21). God desires for His glory and name to be made great throughout the world, bringing society back to a place of right standing with Him. When he sent Jesus to the world as Savior, He presented that opportunity to be made right with Him (God) through Christ. Though the world that once knew no sin has turned from God, you are being called to point people back to Him, one friend at a time.

Scripture Readings

Genesis 6, 7,8 Joshua 1:1-5

Thought of the Day

"In a Good World Gone Bad, you are called to live out God's original intent for our life. A life that reflects and strives to be like Christ."

Questions: (for thought or discussion)

- Have you ever been told to do something that would cause you to look crazy like Noah, but you followed what God said? If so, what and how did it make you feel when following God won you favor?
- In what ways can you contribute to God's original plan as opposed to this *Good World Gone Bad*? What does a separated life look like?
- What would be your "#1" fear in stepping out and being bold as described in Joshua 1:1-5?
- Do you believe God can use what you have done wrong and how you have been forgiven as a tool to help those who are currently struggling? How so?

Today's Challenge

Dedicate thirty (30) minutes to pray for courage to be bold for God.

Day 4

Don't Stop Believing

"Even when there was no reason for hope, Abraham kept hoping- believing that he would become the father of many nations. For God had said to him, 'That's how many descendants you will have!' And Abraham's faith did not weaken, even though, at about 100 years of age, he figured his body was as good as dead- and so was Sarah's womb." Romans 4: 18-19

Has someone ever promised you something you could not wait to have and then they never followed through? Certainly, disappointment is not uncommon to man. Everyone experiences disappointment at one time or another in their lives. However, you can rest assured that God is not like man. He will not make a promise and then not come through. He is faithful to do what He has said and no matter how long you spend waiting, it will happen.

Maybe you have some friends in your life you have been praying for because of some bad decisions they have been making. Maybe you have not been doing well in school and are struggling to pass some of your classes. Maybe you look in the mirror and do not like what you see. However, you placed these things at the feet of Jesus, hoping that change would come and up until now you have seen no change. Do you know the same thing happened with Abraham? He was promised a son and it did not look like it was ever going to happen. According to the book of Romans, he had no reason to continue to believe because all of the odds were stacked against him due to his and Sarah's age. Right when it looks like it is over and seems like there is no way God can come through, He does. God is never late and he is never too early. His timing is perfect.

Abraham could have completely given up. You could have completely given up, but just like Abraham something on the inside would not allow it. That "something" is God reminding you that He is faithful and that He will bring his promises to pass. Abraham's story serves as an example that no matter what it looks like, it is always about what "God said". Do not spend another day thinking that it is not going to happen, your friend will never want God, or you will never see an "A" in your algebra class. If God said it, that should be all you need. Trust Him, more than what you see. You have been called to live out what God has said. Do not Stop Believing!

Scripture Readings

2 Corinthians1:20; Luke 8:40-49; Galatians 6:9

"If God said it, why do you doubt? Trust not only His 'will' but also trust His 'way'."

Questions: (for thought or discussion)

- What have you believed God for that you have seen take place in your life?
- What usually keeps you from believing what God has promised you? What is the obstacle that remains in your way? How do you see getting past it?
- Imagine being like the woman who suffered for 12 years. What would have been your response when you seen Jesus? Would you have had hope, believing for healing or would you have dismissed the possibility?

Today's Challenge

Share with a family member something you are currently learning.

The Waiting Period

"This is what the Lord says: 'You will be in Babylon for seventy years. But then I will come and do for you all the good things I have promised, and I will bring you home again. For I know the plans I have for you', says the Lord. 'They are plans for good and not for disaster, to give you a future and a hope. In those days when you pray, I will listen. If you look for me wholeheartedly, you will find me. I will be found by you,' says the Lord. 'I will end your captivity and restore your fortunes. I will gather you out of the nations where I sent you and will bring you home again to your own land." Jeremiah 29:10-14

The promises of God are true and in His timing, they will come to pass. However, just as in every aspect of life, there is a waiting period. Everything that is worth having is also worth waiting for. Although the society in which we live has a "microwave mentality," the reality of life is you cannot time, box, or schedule what God has planned. You can try, but you can be certain that every attempt will fail. The promise that God declared to the children of Israel concerning all of the good things to come required their trust in God's words even when trials and tests created a sense of doubt.

Jeremiah 29 is one of the most quoted scriptures in reference to God being in control and knowing his intent behind everything. However, most people never take a look at the verse before eleven, which states that the children of Israel would be in exile (outside of your comfort zone, in a foreign place, unknown territory, abandoned, feeling forgotten) before God comes to rescue. Does this sound familiar or what? Have you ever had someone tell you, "So, I have good news and I have bad news, which do you want first?" In saying this, you were being prepared in knowing that at some point you would hear something that would not seem favorable. In many ways this is what God was saying to the children of Israel, "There will be a time period where I seem distant, where my hand of provision will seem non-existent but trust me because even in that season my promise remains true."

At this very moment you may be experiencing doubt or even an unfavorable situation, but hold on because in due time God will do just what He said. He is a faithful God and all of his promises are "Yes and Amen" (2 Cor.1:20). What you are experiencing is not for disaster, it is for good. It may not feel good, but it is indeed for your good. Hold on, this is not permanent. This is the *waiting period.*

Scripture Readings

Romans 8:28; Psalm30:5; Isaiah 41:10

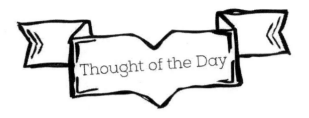

Thought of the Day

*"Having the ability to wait on God, shows
you are ready to receive from God.
Impatience is a clear indicator you have lost
focus in letting God be God in your life."*

Questions: (for thought or discussion)

- What have you waited for that once you received it you found yourself being thankful for the waiting period after all?
- Can you recall a time in your life when you thought your situation would never get better and once it was over, you realized it was not that bad? How did you feel once that season ended?
- What have you waited for the most in your life? Why do you think you have not received it as of yet?

Today's Challenge

*Anonymously leave an encouraging note for
someone in a restaurant.*

Day 6

Created in His Image

"Thank you for making me so wonderfully complex! Your workmanship is marvelous- how well I know it." Psalm 139: 14

From reality TV to music videos to twitter followers, culture has created a false image of reality, beauty, values, and self-esteem. What you see on your screen is a mirror reflection of the emptiness that so much of the world is experiencing. If only the world could see whose image in which it has truly been created. While the world is searching for significance, you as a son or daughter of the King have been given the ability to be a billboard for Christ. His undeniable love and grace, which flows unconditionally, gives you room to reflect that to the world.

There will be people who think you are strange, different or "socially awkward" but guess what!? You are. That's right! You have been set apart to make a difference and you have been set apart to be different. Knowing who you are and whose you are plays a major role in realizing that you were not created to fit in. Throughout the Bible we see young people taking a stand for truth. You are no different. You have not been created to be a clone or to spend your entire life wearing a mask to please people. You were created to live your life, pleasing God. Do not allow yourself to become distracted and diluted with false images of reality.

Open your eyes to the wonderful splendor and gift that looks back at you in the mirror. You have been created in the image of the King and how greatly loved you are by Him. You may feel like you have made some bad decisions. That you will never forgive yourself, but will you allow God to rescue you from the guilt and shame? He knew exactly what He was doing when He created you. He knows every sin, flaw, and hiccup that you have experienced along the way and yet, He still calls you His child. He takes pride in being you Father. He delights in you right where you are. Do no spend not another day searching for your identity. You were created to be a "Child of God" and you were born with purpose.

The same people who called me "different" or "deep" are the same people that voted me prom queen in my High school days and are the same people that I counsel today. Do not be fooled by what people say, deep inside they admire and respect you. As a teenager your peers will not know how to tell you, but know this; "They are watching". You are making a difference and the fact that you are *Living out Loud in a Silent World*" causes them to think about the God you serve and love. Do not allow rejection to stop you from being you, do not allow rejection to motivate you to live like everyone else. You were *created in His Image.*

Scripture Readings

Psalm 139:13-18; Ephesians 2:10, 1 Peter 2:9

"You have been created to be set aside, admired, and seen as a Billboard for the King."

Questions: (for thought or discussion)

- How did you feel when you hear what God thinks of you Psalm 139?
- What do you feel brings the greatest worth and value to your life? What do you feel you offer the world as a result of being God's masterpiece?
- What stops you from being you? What mask are you wearing to belong?

Today's Challenge

Write down three (3) areas of your life you are giving to God.

Day 7

What do you need?

"The Lord is my shepherd; I have all that I need." Psalm 23:1

Do you really feel that you lack or are in need? Really, think about this. People around the world, including your city, neighborhood, country, and world are living below the poverty level. At least this is what the news media declares. However, one must ask what the definition of "poverty" is. Is poverty not being able to eat three or four times a day? Is poverty not having a vehicle? Is poverty not being able to see a doctor? What exactly is poverty? How can one explain the mindset and smile that is often seen on the faces of children and adults around the world who have the bare minimum, or even less. Could it be that what you need is what you have? Or could it be that the defining factor of need changes from one person, country, or culture to the next?

These questions are real and relevant but today as you participate in the scripture reading, you must ask yourself, "Have I acknowledged God as my shepherd? Or do I seek him when I do not have what I want?" David opens this chapter with the premise of God being the source and the provider of everything needed in life. But, if that is the case, what is the state that people find themselves in, if all that is needed is found in God? Understanding what God desires to do in your life and what He desires to add to your life is key. If you are unaware of God's provision or help, then it will be a challenge to see that what you need, what you have. I have had various personal conversations concerning God being a provider and explaining the depth of poverty. The underlying factor remaining in every conversation is that "No matter what you feel like you are lacking, you are still alive to tell about it".

You may say to yourself that just because you are alive does not mean that you have no lack. However, the fact of being in lack would mean to be missing what one needs to live. That you are still alive, is an indicator you are not missing anything essential to live. This may seem like a mind blowing concept, but as you are invited *to live out loud in a silent world*, you must be willing to step out of the box the world has created. Despite what you feel you need, you are clearly surviving without the things you thought you needed. You are able to survive without them. God is taking care of you above and beyond what you could ever imagine, so open your eyes to see his many blessings. As a matter of fact, try to count all that God has done. I guarantee if you did that, I would be reading your upcoming book.

Your life is a reflection of God's thoughts of you and the beauty and boldness he sees when He looks at you! Do not allow yourself to become worried or sad because of what you see other people gaining. What do you need that you cannot live without? That you do not have? Nothing. You are living at this very moment, which proves the life giving Spirit of God lives on the inside of you. You are more alive and more blessed than you could ever imagine. God is your shepherd and the love He has for you is a reflection of what you see each and every day. So, the next time you part your lips to complain of what you do not have that you think you need, begin to thank God instead for what He has already provided.

Scripture Readings

Psalm 23, 119:36-37; Proverbs 10:2; Philippians 4:19

"All of your needs have been supplied, so what is the purpose behind what you want?"

Questions: (for thought or discussion)

- Did you feel challenged in having to acknowledge you are not lacking what you need? What were your feelings after reading the scriptures?
- What has God given you that you have not properly thanked Him for?
- According to Psalm 119: 36-37, life is given through God's word, what does that mean to you?
- What do you feel you lack at this moment in your life? Are you really in lack or just lacking what you want?

Write one journal entry about what life in Christ means to you.

Day 8

Prison Praise

*"Around midnight Paul and Silas were praying
and singing hymns to God, and the other
prisoners were listening. Suddenly, there was a
massive earthquake, and the prison was
shaken to its foundation. All the doors
immediately fell off!" Acts 16:25-26*

Have you ever planned to give someone a really nice gift, but because of an argument you either kept it for yourself or returned it, then gave them something of lesser value? Chances are in some way this has happened. The situation may look a little different, but the fact is something that was to be done or said was held back. I often classify this as holding things "hostage". This response is often given when something is desired based only on favorable circumstances. In the book of Acts, Paul and Silas made the decision to not hold their praise hostage, but to give God "unconditional" worship while in prison.

Maybe you have found yourself holding your attendance in church, prayer life, or devotion to God hostage because negative things were happening in your life, but be aware that you are only delaying the blessings that God desires to give. No matter what happens there is a God who *Runs the World* that desires your praise and is worthy of it. Do not allow the enemy, who is the devil to ruin what God has allowed for his glory and for your good.

God was able to turn a bad situation in to a good situation because of Paul and Silas' obedience and heart. It may be possible that the reason you feel stuck where you are is because of a lack of praise and honor you should be giving to God. Try praising God before you see your test score or before you hear the response of your parents concerning a "not so great" decision you made. You will be surprised at how praise (your response) can change things. Who knows what Paul and Silas were singing or praying but one thing is for sure, it moved God and drew his attention!

The amazing fact in this account is that not only did Paul and Silas's praise give them freedom, it also freed the people around them. Your praise (response) is being watched by people around you. Be careful that your response is not keeping people stuck, but presenting a way of escape. You have it in you! Believe in yourself. Believe in him who will give you strength.

Prison praise will cause walls to come down even if you have been disappointed by an absent parent, failed class, divorced parents, or low self-esteem. You have freedom on the inside of you and you will receive by giving God praise even when you feel discouraged. Prison praise will break the chains, and set you free. Freedom from the thoughts of your peers, bullies, and even siblings belongs to you. Begin to praise God in advance for what he has done and watch what He does!

Scripture Readings

Acts 16:16-30; 1 Thessalonians 5:18; Psalm 150:6; Philippians 4:6

Thought of the Day

"Do not allow the "prison" to take your praise. Allow your praise to take over your prison. Freedom from your prison (situation) is locked up in your praise."

Questions: (for thought or discussion)

- What has been a prison in your life that has tried to stop you from praying and praising God?
- Can you think of a time where your response helped someone else because they were experiencing the same thing?
- Recall a situation that changed because of your prayers and praise to God. How did you feel knowing God was on your side even in a challenging time?
- How can you use your "prison" as a tool to share Jesus?

Today's Challenge

Stand up for someone that is being bullied.

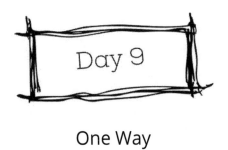

One Way

> *"No, we don't know, Lord,' Thomas said. 'We have no idea where you are going, so how can we know the way?' Jesus told him, 'I am the way, the truth, and the life. No one can come to the Father except through me." John 14:5-6*

In a culture where life is all about keeping your options open, Jesus steps on the scene teaching and demonstrating the very opposite. He did not say to Thomas that he is "a way," but that he is "the way", leaving no room for misunderstanding, misinterpretation or doubt. Jesus makes it perfectly clear that in order to find direction, one must seek and follow him. As a youth, you will have to make a decision to take a stand for Christ. At some point this may even mean you have to stand alone, walk alone, and even experience certain things alone. However, God promises he will never leave.

The only way to live for Christ is to actually live for Christ. This is a daily choice to say "yes" to God and "no" to the world. According to 2 Timothy 3:12 there will be persecution (hard times, people who disagree with you) because of your decision to say yes to God. Keep in mind that what you gain in Christ pales in comparison to what you let go of in this world. Sure, there will be days where you want to hang out with friends and do what you used to do. However, Holy Spirit who is a leader and guide will provide you with the needed strength.

Jesus wanted to make it clear for Thomas that he was not going to lead him astray and for as long as he followed Jesus, Thomas would be exactly where he was needed. True life is found in Christ. The truth most of your friends are searching for is found in a life given over to God. When you made the decision to say "yes" to Jesus, a door was opened. A door that gives you access to hope, peace, love, joy and everything that is good, pleasing and perfect. Jesus doesn't want to be another decision you make. He wants to be the only decision that you make.

The life made available to you reflects all that the world is looking for. You have the key that can unlock the doors in your peers' lives. Those friends who have come to you with their problems are searching for truth and that truth is found in Christ. May you be bold and vocal to express and live a life that points people to Christ? Your "yes" to Jesus is bigger than you realize, it will be the hope that others are looking for.

Scripture Readings

Colossians 3:3; Matthew 5:14-16; Matthew 7:7-8

Thought of the Day

"Jesus desires not be an option, but to be your only choice."

Questions: (for thought or discussion)

- What does it mean for you to make Jesus your only way?
- Define a life that is hidden in Christ. What does the "hidden" life look like to you?
- In what ways can you be a light at school, work or even with your friends?

Today's Challenge

Invite a friend to youth group or Bible Study.

Day 10

Add a Little Flavor

"You are the salt of the earth. But what good is salt if it has lost its flavor? Can you make it salty again? It will be thrown out and trampled underfoot as worthless." Matthew 5:13 (NIV)

Salt is a preservative used to maintain or keep alive that which has the possibility of dying. In this scripture Jesus is saying, that is what you, as a child of God, have been called to do. You are a substance (light, flavor) added to the world to keep the world from dying without Jesus Christ. How amazing is this? You are able to add flavor to a world that has diluted the truth and has turned a deaf ear to God. It is time to add flavor to your school, your friendships, your basketball teams, and even your family.

Do not believe the lie that you are too young. God has set you aside. Just like yesterday's scripture readings, your life has been hidden in Christ. You must be sure that your life is hidden in Christ and not hidden from Christ. In order to keep alive and maintain the environment you are in you must speak out. Live your life so loud the people around you cannot help but acknowledge the existence of God in you. It can be a challenge to be bold for God when you are surrounded by friends who do not know him. Do not let that stop you. Let it motivate you to be a witness.

The greatest witness you have is your personal story of how God changed your life when you accepted his son. Your friends want to know you are serious. Not serving God today and doubting him tomorrow. The consistency of your relationship with God, your constant communication with Him will represent the value you place in Him. If you value your relationship with Him, you will desire to be in constant relation/communication. This means you will spend as much time with God as you see fit. The more you grow in love with God, the more you will spend time with him. Your friends are watching to see if this is just a phase or if you are really serious. Your actions will prove to them how serious you are.

If your life loses its flavor, what use are you to the Kingdom of God? Do not become watered down in an attempt to fit in! You are a display of hope; flavor that is added to give life, and an inspiration to those around you! Because of Christ you have the flavor the world is looking for.

Scripture Readings

Titus 2:11-14; Matthew 5:16; Proverbs 22:1

Thought of the Day

"Do not lose your flavor because the world is trying to water you down. Add flavor everywhere you go. You are the inspiration people are looking for."

Questions: (for thought or discussion)

- What does it mean to you to add flavor to the world? How can you add flavor in your environment every day?
- What are the key obstacles challenging you in being bold for Jesus?
- Do you think that you can add flavor to your conversations with friends who do not know God? How so?

Have a Bible Study with a few friends at your house.

Day 11

Don't be moved

"Shadrach, Meshach, and Abednego replied, 'O Nebuchadnezzar, we do not need to defend ourselves before you. If we are thrown into the blazing furnace, the God whom we serve is able to save us. He will rescue us from your power, Your Majesty. But even if he doesn't, we want to make it clear to you, Your Majesty, that we will never serve your gods or worship the gold statue you have set up." Daniel 3:17-18

The blazing furnace may be your friends disowning you; talking about you on Facebook; not allowing you to sit with them at lunch; creating horrible rumours about you; or even tweeting about your decision to not bow to this world. The "heat" is turned up in many different ways and can happen anywhere. However, just like the three Hebrew boys who were willing to stand in the face of the enemy, they remained strong and immovable. God has also given you that ability. You may not always feel that way. You may not always want to respond in a bold manner, but keep in mind that the one who lives inside of you is greater than the world.

These three boys were willing to risk it all for God. They believed God was able to come to their rescue and even if he did not it would not change their stance for the one and true living God. At some point there will be a friend or maybe even a stranger who will want you to do something that goes against what you believe. You will have to think very carefully about your decision. Shadrach, Meshach, and Abednego valued their commitment and devotion to God more than their own lives. Not everyone is able or willing to take that stand, but these boys sure were.

Can you think of a time in your life where you stood up for what you believed and it cost you something? How do you feel when you look back at how bold you were? Do you feel powerful or strong because you chose the right thing even though other people did not agree? People will certainly not agree with every decision you make, especially when you make good decisions for God. People will try to tear you down. Keeping in mind that God is with you through it all is important. During your scripture reading you will see how God rescues Shadrach, Meshach, and Abednego. He comes just in time and as result of their amazing choice, others heard of how God showed up.

The choice you make in standing up for God will not only benefit you, but it will bring other people into the knowledge of who God is and what He is able to do. Do not be moved by what it looks like, be empowered by your God.

Scripture Readings

Daniel 3; 1 Peter 4:12; 2 Chronicles 20:15; Romans 8:31

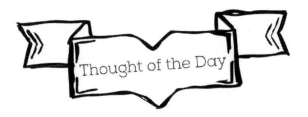

"Do not be worried about who is against you, be encouraged because of Him who is with you."

Questions: (for thought or discussion)

- Can you recall a time when God came to rescue at just the right time? How did you feel knowing you were not alone?
- If you were King Nebuchadnezzar what would you have done when you saw Shadrach, Meshach, and Abednego walking around in the furnace?
- When have you felt the most protected by God? What was going on in your life?
- Have you ever felt like God was not there, but then you realized he was the one who helped you with your problem? It was Him not you!

Today's Challenge

Ask your leader at church if you could share your story some time.

Day 12

The Temple

---

*"God's will is for you to be holy, so stay away
from all sexual sin. Then each of you will
control his own body and live in holiness and
honor- not in lustful passion like the pagans
who do not know God and his ways."*
1 Thessalonians 4:3-5

When God created you, He did so with the original
intent of your life to be a living testimony of His love, grace,
and purity. Your body is a temple that should be honored
and respected because you are a child of the King. You are
not common. You are not an after-thought. God knew
exactly what he was doing when he created you. He did not
make a single mistake. However, the enemy who is out to kill,
still, and destroy (John 10:10) distorts the truth by
presenting sex before marriage as the normal way of life and
it is not. Your body was meant to be shared with one man or
one woman. Though the world teaches differently, your
body was not created as a "free for all."

According to 1 Corinthians 7:23, God paid a high price
for you so you would not have to stay stuck or a slave to sin.
The high price he paid was the blood of his son Jesus Christ.
He paid this price so you would know how loved you are no

matter what you have done. God desires to free you from every decision and every mistake that makes you feel like you are not good enough. Your body is a gift and treasure that is to be given to God until marriage. This may be a challenge, but God is your strength and with Him all things are possible.

The world has constructed an image defining our beauty and worth as having "sex" appeal, making it cool when in reality is has just the opposite effect. Think of when you are older and stand at the altar to marry the person you love. But, all you can think about are the other people who you gave your body to. If you have made decisions to give your body to someone, take it back and give it to the rightful owner—God. It is not too late to make a change. You can make the decision right now. Maybe you have not been impure with someone, maybe it is inappropriate things that you watch on TV or magazines that you find entertaining. Maybe you have had conversations that were not pleasing to God. Make the decision today to give all of those challenges to God. Give him room to work in and through you. He is able to change your desires. He is able to make you new. He is able to do what you cannot do for yourself. Your body is a temple God desires to live in, but He can only do that as you allow him to make you new and clean.

Scripture Readings

1 Corinthians 10:12-13, James 4:7; 2Timothy 2:20-22; Romans 12:1-2

"Your body is a temple God desires to live in. May your actions be a reflection of God living inside of you."

Questions: (for thought or discussion)

- What does honouring God with your body mean to you?
- How important is it for you to set boundaries with your boy/girl friendships?
- Can you remember a time in your life where you resisted temptation and God protected you as a result of it? If so, how did He protect you?
- Have you ever given a friend advice concerning boundaries? Have you been able to use personal experiences to help them understand?
- According to Psalm 119:9, instructions are given as to how a young person can stay pure. What is your response? Do you feel that God's word helps you stay pure? If so, How? If not, Why?

Challenge yourself to spend one (1) hour with God in prayer for boldness.

This is not Your Home

"Dear friends, I warn you as 'temporary residents and foreigners' to keep away from worldly desires that wage war against your very souls. Be careful to live properly among your unbelieving neighbors." 1 Peter 2:11-12a

---

Have you ever seen a movie where the husband comes home from work, opens the front door and says, "Honey, I'm home?" Chances are you have. But, let's say for an example, the husband walked into a home that was not his, hung his coat up, propped his feet on the coffee table and said those same words. Would that be strange? Of course it would. It would be strange and random because he has walked into a home that is not his and has become, "Oh so comfortable."

In many ways this is what is done daily. This place called "earth" is temporary. Just as Peter warns God's people against worldly desires, he also calls them temporary residents. This indicates that where we are is not our final destination. God is preparing a home that cannot be imagined, beauty that has never been seen, and splendor that is out of this world. How very important it is to monitor our responses and the way we live our lives because what is done here plays a major role in what is to come. You are children of the light, being called out of darkness. In fact, as you are being called to live life in the light, you are also being called to live life, "lightly". This is placing struggles, problems, and worry at the feet of Jesus.

There are peers all around who do not believe, but are watching your every move. That is right, people are watching to see if you will stay true to God or if you will fall into the temptations of this world. Will you prove them wrong? Will you live your life so loud that there is no room for doubt or question? You have it on the inside, but the question is not do you have it. The question is what will you do with what you have? Do not keep quiet. Stop trying to blend it. It is okay that you are not from here. You are just passing through as a visitor to carry out the plan God has for your life.

God has given you freedom to choose daily and with the exercise of that freedom, people will either be encouraged by your decisions or they will be lost as a result. This may seem like a huge deal, but that is only because it is. You are a big deal in the Kingdom of God. Your life and the decisions that you make in this temporary home could not be more important! Be wise and do not get too comfortable. God is preparing a better place.

Scripture Readings

1 John 5:21, 2:15-17; Hebrews 11: 13-19; 1Corinthians 10:33; John 13:1-3

"Be careful not to build a house on property that you do not own."(Do not get too comfortable, or too worried about life's troubles because what you are experiencing is only temporary.

Questions: (for thought or discussion)

- What does it mean to live this life as a temporary one? What would that look like in terms of friendships, stress, gossip, etc?
- Do you believe you are accountable to live a life that helps others and points them to Jesus?
- Will you continue to believe God for what He has said, no matter how long it takes?
- What are your thoughts of Heaven? Do the thoughts of Heaven make you excited, nervous, etc? Why?

Give something precious away. (Consider what could be a blessing to someone.)

Day 14

Got Fruit?

---

*"But the Holy Spirit produces this kind of fruit
in our lives: love, joy, peace, patience, kindness,
goodness, faithfulness, gentleness, and self-
control. There is no law against these things!"*
Galatians 5:22 - 23

Have you ever looked at an apple tree, seen the apples and wondered if that tree could produce oranges as well? Probably not. In the same way your life has been designed to be like that of a tree. The fruit you bear will clearly identify and distinguish you from other trees and fruit. So, if there is no fruit, this can also be an indicator of who you are. In the same way than an apple tree cannot bear oranges and grapes is just how your life will only produce fruit after its own kind, just like God designed.

If the Holy Spirit produces amazing fruit in the lives of those who have accepted Jesus but yet the fruit is seldom seen, one must consider the role that you have personally given to Holy Spirit. Have you given Holy Spirit the room to guide, lead, and also convict or have you reserved his services only for Sunday? Whatever you feed will grow and whatever you starve will die. You can either feed yourself by what you allow in and by what you personally deposit in your one-on-one time with God. In this same way, you can either starve yourself in terms of the fruit of the Spirit by allowing negativity in your life.

The wonderful benefit of living your life as a good fruit bearing tree is that those who are struggling, those who need encouragement, and those who need help can come to you. However, if your tree is fruitless you miss out and others whom you could have helped will as well. It is important that you realize in your youth how the decisions you make or do not make affect you and those around you. You have been called out of this world to be a light in the midst of darkness, to be a voice in the silence, to be hope for those who have none. This is the life you have been called to live, but how can you give to others, when you have nothing to give. Your life is a tree, make sure you are taking out the time to water your tree with the Word of God, Worship and Prayer. You need fruit and others need it to!

Scripture Readings

Galatians 6:7; Matthew 17:15-20; Luke 6:45; Philippians 4:8

"A tree is known by the fruit that it bears.
What are you known for?"

Questions: (for thought or discussion)

- Recall a time in your life where you wanted to say something but you did not because God would not let the words come out. How did it make you feel, knowing that those negative words you used to say would no longer come out? Did you feel like true change had taken place?
- How did it feel the first time you chose to be kind to someone who was not kind to you? Were you surprised by your actions?
- Do you find that the more you spend time with God, the more at peace you are? Give some examples.

Today's Challenge

Talk to your family about your goals (have them hold you accountable).

Day 15

The Voice of God

---

*"Go out and stand before me on the mountain,'
the Lord told him. And as Elijah stood there,
the Lord passed by, and a mighty windstorm
hit the mountain. It was such a terrible blast
that the rocks were torn loose, but the Lord
was not in the wind. After the wind there was
an earthquake, but the Lord was not in the
earthquake. And after the earthquake there
was a fire, but the Lord was not in the fire. And
after the fire there was the sound of a gentle
whisper."* 1 Kings 19: 11-12

What were you expecting? Fire? Wind? Rain? Snow?
Thunder? Can God speak in this way? He sure can. Does he
always speak in a big and loud way? No. The challenge in
learning to hear God's voice is being able to quiet yourself
from fear, distractions and self. The *Prayer Posture Model* that
is listed in the back teaches how to be still in the presence of
God. God desires to talk to you. He wants you to hear him
speak. He does not want it to be a mystery; he wants to make
himself known. However, the key in understanding the voice
of God is remembering that most of the time, it will not be
what you are expecting and it probably will not be the way

you are imagined. He may speak to you through an image, nature, a song, through a friend or even in a feeling. God has no limitations, so expand your thoughts of who He is!

In 1 Kings God spoke in a still, small whisper, not in a big bang. There are many reasons why God spoke this way. But, the lesson to be learned is how Elijah was able to identify God's voice. It is not about how God speaks, it is about recognizing his voice. God speaks daily but many times distractions get in the way of hearing his voice clearly. Today, challenge yourself to take some quiet time just for you and God. Let go of the day. Let go of what happened and just wait on Him. There are endless possibilities of what one moment in His presence can do.

The world may not understand why or how you talk with God, but as you live your life out loud, the world will begin to see God living in you. Get ready, because people will have questions, so you will need to spend time in God's presence seeking him for wisdom and boldness to represent Him. Do not miss what God is saying to you because it is not what you planned or what you imagined. Many people missed Jesus as he walked through various villages and towns because he did not look how they imagined. Many people did not believe he was the Son of God and they missed their up-close and personal opportunity to be with him. Do not miss your opportunity to hear from God because of a lack of patience or fear of the unknown. The best conversation you will ever have is with God! Take some time today and just hang out with him. Go to the park with a devotional. Bring your Bible, and just wait on Him.

Scripture Readings

John 10:27-28; Isaiah 28:23

Thought of the Day

"If you want to hear the voice of God turn off everything that has a volume knob. This may be the TV, iPod, cell phone etc. God wants your undivided attention."

Questions: (for thought or discussion)

- Have you ever heard the voice of God? What was it like?
- Do you ever have dreams and feel like God was trying to get your attention? What was your response?
- Do you think God can use someone else to relay a message to you? Has this ever happened?
- Can you recall any time where God spoke but you did not listen? And later realized that God was trying to help but you ignored him? How can you prevent that from happening again?
- How can you help friends understand that God desires to speak to them?

Today's Challenge

Offer inbox prayer on Facebook. Make yourself available for the needs of others.

Day 16

Face Your Giant

"As Goliath moved closer to attack, David quickly ran out to meet him. Reaching into his shepherd's bag and taking out a stone, he hurled it with his sling and hit the Philistine in the forehead. The stone sank in, and Goliath stumbled and fell face down on the ground." 1 Samuel 17:48 -49

There is a giant that every person must face. A giant that tries to steal, kill, and destroy. This giant is the devil and he will try any and every thing to convince you that he will win. However, be encouraged; the end has already been written and guess what! You win. You come out on top. Despite your friends making fun of you; despite you having low self-esteem; despite being put down over and over again, you made it. The enemy did not win and no matter who he used to try and attack you, you are still here.

It is not enough to acknowledge that your giant exists. You must face that giant as well. According to Philippians 4:13 you can do all things through Christ. With God on your side, you always win. You may not always feel like a winner. You may not always look like a winner. But, as long as you are God's team, you always win. David was just a boy when he fought Goliath. His own family counted him out and did not encourage him but he was convinced it was his time. He was not moved by what his family said or the height of Goliath because he knew the height of his God.

As you live each day as loud as you can there will be giants trying to shut you up. There will be giants that come at school, work and friendships but from the time you accepted Jesus in your heart, all needed to win every battle came into your possession. Just as David quickly ran to fight Goliath, you too can stand before your giant of low self-esteem, drugs, alcohol, peer pressure, or whatever with confidence, declaring who you are in God. Just as Goliath fell to the ground, believe yours will also.

Scripture Readings

1 Samuel 17; Jeremiah 1:19

Look your giant in the face and say, "Are you ready to meet defeat? (d-feet) because I'm about to kick you to the curb."

Questions: (for thought or discussion)

- What has been your biggest giant? How did you fight it?
- What is your best weapon against your giants? What helps you to remember you are not fighting alone?

- How do you deal with people saying you are too young to win against big giants or hard problems? Do you find yourself being motivated to really fight when people doubt you? Or do you feel discouraged to even try?
- What are three (3) tools you could use daily to fight against the giants that come?

Step out on faith and offer prayer with your friends at your lunch table.

Day 17

All things New

"This means that anyone who belongs to Christ has become a new person. The old life is gone; a new life has begun! And all of this is a gift from God, who brought us back to himself through Christ. And God has given us this task of reconciling the world to himself, no longer counting people's sin against them". 2 Corinthians 5: 17-18

Each and every day God continues to love you right where you are. When you said yes to him, you opened your heart and you entire life to the plan God has for you. You are no longer stuck with the "old you". You are free from what you did, what you said, and who you used to be. Jesus came to make all things new and He makes this new life available at the very moment you say yes to him! There are no surprises with God. His love for you in unconditional and you are able to receive that love.

Have you made changes in your life that have turned you into a completely different person, but your friends will not let you forget the bad decisions that you made "B.C" (Before Christ)? Everyone has those kinds of people who try to keep another from moving forward with God. However, you must keep in mind that you are no longer that person, and the guilt that tries to come and taunt you is not from God, it is from the enemy. Your new life in Christ is a billboard for the entire world to see how with God all things are possible.

There may be days where you feel like you are not good enough, but as you read the scriptures for the day, you will see that we are not saved by works, we are saved by grace. There is nothing you could do that could make God love you less. He loves you knowing every secret and every hidden desire of your heart and he still calls you his child. Do not allow who you used to be to stop you from becoming who God has purposed for you to be. You are free from the chains of sin, and your freedom is a daily decision you must choose.

God sent his son Jesus to the world so we might be reconnected with him. God desires that no one would perish (2 Peter 3:9). He is faithful to turn your life around and every bad habit, desire, or thought can be changed with God. Change is an ongoing process and you must lay your ideas down and welcome the plan of God daily. You are new, leave the old behind.

Scripture Readings

Romans 7, 8; Revelation 21:5; Ephesians 2:9; 1 John 3:7-10

Thought of the Day

"Do not stay stuck in who you were. Identify yourself by who you are now."

Questions: (for thought or discussion)

- How does it make you feel to know you are forgiven from every bad choice and decision you have made?
- How can you show your friends that you are no longer the same? Is it a challenge? How do you feel when they say the "new you" is boring?
- How would you explain to your friends that having a relationship with God is not about works, but grace? What would be your definition of grace?
- What are some aspects of your "old life" that try to get you to come back? How do you fight the temptation?

Today's Challenge

Ask a friend if there is something that you could pray for, for them.

Day 18

Stop, Drop, and Roll

*"One day as Jesus was walking along the shore
of the Sea of Galilee, he saw Simon and his
brother Andrew throwing a net into the water,
for they fished for a living. Jesus called out to
them, 'Come, follow me, and I will show you
how to fish for people!' And they left their nets
at once and followed him." Mark 1:16-18*

Have you ever been told do something right away and
your response was, "I will, just give me a minute?" Sure you
have. There is something about not wanting to do something
at the moment we are told. Maybe, it has something to do
with wanting to be in control and wanting to do it at our own
pace. However, look at Simon and Andrew who were out
fishing. They were doing what they loved and also provided
them with an income. Jesus spots them and calls out to them.
Neither one of them asks a question, hesitates, or ignores the
calling of Jesus. They immediately stop what they are doing,
drop what they have, and roll out. They did not say, "Jesus,
I'm kind of busy. This is how I make my money and support
my family." No, they listened and responded.

As a youth, you will be pulled in many directions, but
it is very important to make sure you do not miss the calling

of God because you are busy doing your "own thing". Not only did Jesus tell them to come follow him, he also assured them that what He was offering would be better than what they had. The life God is leading you to live, while the world becomes increasingly more silent, is one that will stir teenagers all around the world to say "yes" to God. It only takes one person to step out of the box and follow God's leading.

Maybe you have planned your entire life out. Where you will live; the job you will have, and the person you will marry. Can I inform you that more times than not God's plan looks completely different? His plan does not look different because he does not want you happy. His plan looks different because he is the only one who can truly provide what you are looking for. We can only imagine that Andrew and Simon looked at each other and said, "Hey, if he (Jesus) wants to show us something, we need to go check it out." You will not read how they eventually went back to their old lives because when Jesus invites you to live life with him, there is no turning back.

Only you know where you are, what you are doing, and what you look to for financial help. All you could possibly want is found in Christ. Do not be so consumed with what you are doing you fail to see what you are being led to and what you are being led away from. There is more, but you must be willing to *stop, drop, and roll!*

Scripture Readings

Ephesians 5:1; Luke 10:27

"When God calls you the only suitable response is to stop, drop, and roll. There is no time for excuses or delays, just go."

Questions: (for thought or discussion)

- What is the greatest sacrifice you have made for God? What have you been willing to stop for the sake of His call!?
- Do you believe you can follow God and follow your plan? How so?
- If your friends asked you why you stopped doing certain things, what would your response be? What does stop, drop, and roll mean to you?

Write down what you feel have been noticeable changes in your life.

Day 19

It's Your Time

"Don't let anyone think less of you because you are young. Be an example to all believers in what you say, in the way you live, in your love, your faith, and your purity." 1 Timothy 4:12

It is true. Young people are often looked over, now is your time to give people a reason to look at you again. Your life speaks loud and clear of what God can do at any age. Even though your friends will try to stop you, keep going. In this life you have no limits, outside of what you create but with God limits do not exist. You are just about at the half way mark of your forty day journey. Look at all the goals you have set, the scriptures you have fed yourself, and the people you have inspired. If you would have waited another 10 years can you imagine what you would have missed out on in your youth?

Now is your time to show the world that God is using young people who dare to be different, stand for what is right, and will not back down in the face of the enemy. The time has come where change can take place in your schools because of your "yes" to God. What is holding you back from giving your all? Is it your friends, the popular people at school or is it fear? According 2 Timothy 1:7 fear has not been given to you by God, but power, love and a sound mind has. So, right now in this very moment, let go of fear, let go of the lies you have believed about yourself and the fear of not being accepted by people. God is with you and he will see you through every problem.

There are many movies that hit the big screen. The most successful movies are the ones that touch the heart or leave people spellbound. In both instances what is seen, triggers something within. Can you recall the last movie you went to the theater to see that kept you on your toes or you talked about days after? What was it about the movie that "got" you? The way you respond will identify your interest. In the same way, the impression you leave at your school and in your community will also have people talking after you have graduated and moved on. Living out loud in a silent World is about leaving behind a legacy pointing people to Christ everywhere you go. Do not waste another day. It is your time now!

Scripture Readings

John 2:14; Ephesians 5:1-20; Ecclesiastes 12:1; Matthew 18:3

"It is not about what you did yesterday, or what you will do tomorrow. What you do today is what counts."

Questions: (for thought or discussion)

- Why do you think it is important to become devoted to God as a young person?
- What motivates you to live out loud when the world tries to tell you are too young?
- In what ways do you feel your life will be better because of your "Yes" to God as a youth?
- What do you want people to say about you when you are no longer here? What legacy do you want to leave behind?

Pray in a public place.

Day 20

The Dream Lives On

"When Joseph's brothers saw him coming, they recognized him in the distance. As he approached, they made plans to kill him. 'Here comes the dreamer!' they said. 'Come on let's kill him and throw him into one of these cisterns. We can tell our father, A wild animal has eaten him. Then we'll see what becomes of his dreams." Genesis 37:18, 20

As you follow Christ and live out loud there will be people along the way that are set up by the enemy as "dream killers". Dream killers are people who see all what God is doing in and through you. They see you are in love with God and just like the three Hebrew boys; you are not bowing to false gods and this makes them mad. They have been assigned to stop you from believing. Joseph had been given a dream and his brothers did not like the dream or Joseph. They created a plan to see Joseph suffer, but God had a different plan to see Joseph succeed.

Do not worry about the people who are trying to stop what cannot be stopped. Their plan will not work. God knows exactly what he is doing and though their plans against you were for evil God will turn it around for His good. Joseph's brothers were convinced they had seen the last of him. They changed their plans and sold him into slavery, but God was faithful to what he had promised Joseph. As you will see in your scripture reading for today, Joseph went through a lot before the dream came to pass. There were probably times where he felt like giving up; times where he doubted God; and times where he doubted himself. Maybe God has shown you visions or dreams just like Joseph, but you became discouraged because of what was going on around you. Just as God brought to pass what he said to Joseph, he will also bring to pass what he has said to you.

One of the challenges we have to endure in life is to wait. Waiting seems to be the most draining or prolonged period of life. But, you can be certain of one thing, there is a due season. God is intentional with never being late, and never coming before you are prepared. The dream God has given, the desire on your heart, and the passion you have for what God has revealed will indeed come forth at just the right time. No matter what you experience and no matter what dream killers try to do or say, be encouraged because the *dream lives on!*

Scripture Readings

Genesis 37, 39-45 (chapters)

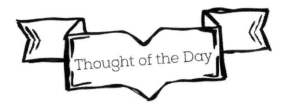

"People may try to stop you, kill you, and even break you, but rest assured that the

dream lives on. What man tries to destroy,
God will exalt."

Questions: (for thought or discussion)

- Is there anything God has revealed to you that people made fun of you for? Most of the time people criticize what they do not understand, but know that God's word always stands.
- What would you have done if you were Joseph? Would you have blessed your brothers or punished them?
- How do you think you would have felt if your family members sold you?
- How can you use Joseph's story as a testimony for those who feel like there is no way God is able to come to the rescue?
- Challenge yourself to do something nice for a person that never says hello. Maybe it is a person in your school or at your bus stop.

Today's Challenge

Share encouraging words with a stranger.

No one is Perfect

"For everyone has sinned; we all fall short of God's glorious standard. Yet God, with underserved kindness, declares that we are righteous. He did this through Christ Jesus when he freed us from the penalty for our sins." Romans 3:23-24

The love God gives cannot be explained. From the very beginning, God chose to love us beyond and above the love we could give him. He knew every mistake that would be made, every hidden secret, and every thought that wanders the minds of men. And yet, He declares his children righteous. It is true no one walking this earth is perfect. However, as children of God and as children of the light, the desire to be like Christ should be the compass or "gps" of your life. There will be days when you get off track, but because you allow God to lead, you can be confident he will place you where to need to be.

Romans chapter 8 states there is no condemnation (guilt) for those who have given their lives to Christ. This means every sin you have committed was nailed to the cross and you are made whole through repentance and God's grace. How amazing is it that God sees all and knows all and chooses to throw all sin into the depths of the sea (Micah 7:19). Your relationship with God is not built on all the things you do right. It is based on all the things you bring before Him. He wants to be your life, not our day, not penciled in your schedule, but your entire life.

God declares you righteous because of the blood of Jesus that was shed for all of humanity. You are part of God's plan to send redemption (right relationship, wholeness) to the world. Your love for God will draw people to Christ. As you live out loud in this silent world, the light of Christ will shed light in the darkness. Eyes will be opened, and friends will have questions and because you are able to testify to God's acceptance of you just as you are, other's will want to know God in the same way. Change and growth comes as you grow in love with God and you seek to please only him. Your lifestyle and actions begin to resemble that relationship. Do not be so hard on yourself. God makes grace available to you and not only when you repent, but when you turn away from wrong doing, God brings healing.

Scripture Readings

Galatians 2:17-21; Isaiah 1:18; Acts 3:19

Thought of the Day

"The Grace of God gives multiple opportunities to be made whole and to be made new."

Questions: (for thought or discussion)

- Define "dying to the law" as described in Galatians 2. How do you carry that out daily?
- How does it make you feel to know you have been freed from the penalty of sin? How can you explain to friends how God loves them even when they make bad decisions? What examples in the Bible would you give?
- How would you explain the process of forgiveness of sin?
- Do you believe God really accepts you as you are? Can you think of something that happened that allowed you to see how he really does accept you?

Today's Challenge

Look for someone in a public place that you can help.

Day 22

Got love?

"Love is patient and kind. Love is not jealous or boastful or proud or rude. It does not demand its own way. It is not irritable, and it keeps no record of being wronged. It does not rejoice about injustice but rejoices whenever the truth wins out. Love never gives up, never loses faith, is always hopeful, and endures through every circumstance." 1 Corinthians 13: 4-7

After reading the defining factors of what true love is, can you say this is what you have or this is what you extend to others? We have all held a grudge at some point, but can you take a moment and consider the many times you have wronged God. And yet, he continually remained with arms wide open. The world is searching for it. People spend their entire lives thinking they have it. And then there are people who die as a result of it. What can be said about the most precious gift God has made available?

Have you ever been really mad at your mom or dad and told them you wish you could have new parents? How do you think that made them feel? Sad, maybe even disappointed? The truth of the matter is not that you really meant it, but that the situation made you mad to the point of wanting something to change. It is interesting because the love God has for you does not change, no matter how many times you fall asleep while you are praying at night, gossip, text during the entire church service or even beg your parent not to make you go. The depth of God's love for you is never altered, tainted, or minimized. In fact, he desires for you to have a heart that allows you to love, not just those who love you, but those who do not.

The world is in a desperate search for love, but not the love according to 1 Corinthians 13. They are searching for an artificial love. Often that artificial love is what is seen in movies, reality TV shows, and captured in music videos. But, what God wants to give you is a love that places a smile on your face when you wake; a love that will think nothing of sacrifice; and a love that allows you to see beyond the outward appearance to reach those who are ignored. What kind of love can you say you give? Is it a love is conditioned by how someone treats you or a love that challenges you to see the best in people on their worst day? *Got Love?*

Scripture Readings

John 13:35; Romans 8:38 -39; John 15:13; 1 John 4:7-21

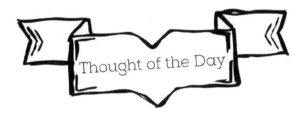

Thought of the Day

"The love of God is far greater than the love of man, but the love of man is great because of the love of God. All you have and all you give is because of Him."

Questions: (for thought or discussion)

- What does 1 Corinthians 13:1-8 look like for your generation? How can you display that love?
- How does Romans 8:38-39 make you feel?
- According to 1 John as you live in God, you live in love and your love grows more perfectly. How do you demonstrate that love? How would define "living in God?"

Today's Challenge

Offer to lead prayer for one week with your family.

Day 23

1

"Dear Children, keep away from anything that might take God's place in your hearts." 1 John 5:21

What would you identify as being an idol? Money, people, clothes, cars? All of these things tend to steal away time and attention God desires. But, what if an idol was not limited to things gained, but is inclusive of things accomplished and goals achieved. Maybe you are an athlete, a rather successful athlete with plaques and trophies. And, every time your friends come over, somehow the conversation shifts to all that you have accomplished. Would you then say that in some respect, what you accomplished has become something you worship?

Take a moment and think about something you have accomplished that makes you feel really good. Got it? Now, take a moment and consider how often you view that accomplishment as a part of your identity. You see, it can be easy to begin finding worth and value in what you have accomplished and placing those things on pedestals as if they have made you who you are. This scripture is not just saying, "Keep bad things away." This scripture is saying be sure that no matter what you have or what you have accomplished your identity is rooted and grounded in the one who lives in your heart.

Sure, it is okay to appreciate, be excited as well as proud of what you have accomplished or even gained. However, be careful to always be mindful that every good and perfect gift comes from God. The enemy's plan is not to stop the world from acknowledging God altogether. His plan is to silence the world in their stance in giving all glory to God and take away for what they believe. He does not care that you believe. He cares that what you believe speaks above and beyond a belief system or religion. The enemy's plan is to ultimately distract and dilute the world with artificial gain because he knows that when God has his rightful place in our lives, he's in trouble.

Live your life with your eyes wide open. Open to the people and things that make you lose sight of your first love, who is Jesus Christ. The scripture does not say there cannot be other things in your life that are important. What the Bible says is that those other things should not be more important than God. Keep things in perspective!

Scripture Readings

James 1:17; Luke 10:27

"Never give more praise to the gift than what you give to the giver."

Questions: (for thought or discussion)

- What is the # 1 thing that tries to steal God's place in your life (generation)?

- How do you maintain focus on God when everything else around you seems interesting too?
- How do you feel when you have not given God all of your attention or your time? Do you feel down? Does it seem like nothing goes right? Do you notice?

Leave a note of encouragement on someone's windshield.

Be on the Look Out

"Therefore, put on every piece of God's armor so you will be able to resist the enemy in the time of evil. Then after the battle you will still be standing firm. Stand your ground, putting on the belt of truth and the body armor of God's righteousness. For shoes, put on the peace that comes from the Good News so that you will be fully prepared. In addition to all of these, hold up the shield of faith to stop the fiery arrows of the devil. Put on salvation as your helmet, and take the sword of the Spirit, which is the word of God." Ephesians 6:13-17

Living out loud in a Silent World is more than what you say; it includes what you do as well. The battle that is going on for your attention, your soul, your voice, and your power in the Kingdom is bigger than you could imagine. John 10:10 captures what the enemy has come to do. Knowing that he wants to steal, kill, and destroy, you must be prepared with your full armor on because it is with spiritual weapons that the enemy is defeated. On Day 8 you learned about *Prison Praise*, the ability to praise God in a low place. This kind of praise is also a spiritual weapon that confuses the enemy.

There are people right now at your school who are struggling with suicide, depression, homosexuality, self-injury, an abusive home life, and all sorts of situations. These are attacks of the enemy. From this day forward you are being challenged to have a listening ear to those around you. To have a ready word that will bring life to those who feel broken and alone. The armor you are to wear daily is a "prepared mindset" that keeps you focused on the truth of God's power and might. Every aspect of your life is covered in the armor of the Lord and the moment you think you do not need it, is the moment you do.

The enemy is crafty, cunning and very subtle. Having your armor on at all times is a must. *Be on the lookout* for people who are trying to start trouble, friends that are gossiping, or any other random encounter that causes you to feel under spiritual attack (an attack that may not be physical, but is affecting your faith or relationship with God).

Scripture Readings

1 Peter 5:8; Deuteronomy 28:7; John 15:18 -19

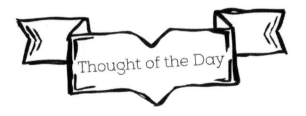

"God did not say you would have no enemies, but he did say you will triumph against them. Do not worry, you are on the winning team."

Questions: (for thought or discussion)

- What is the number one thing that tries to steal God's place in your life (generation)?
- Have you experienced spiritual attack (an attack specifically against your relationship with God)? If so, how do you fight against that attack?
- How would translate "putting on the armor" for someone who does not know about God? What does putting on the armor look like for you?

Spend one (1) day without social media, television, or cell phone.

Day 25

Born to Lead

"Be strong and courageous, for you are the one who will lead these people to possess all the land I swore to their ancestors I would give them. Be strong and very courageous. Be careful to obey all the instructions Moses gave you. Do not deviate from them, turning either to the right or to the left. Then you will be successful in everything you do. Study this Book of Instruction continually. Meditate on it day and night so you will be sure to obey everything written in it. Only then will you prosper and succeed in all you do. This is my command—be strong and courageous! Do not be afraid or discouraged. For the Lord your God is with you wherever you go." Joshua 1:6-10

If there is one thing the Lord is making clear to young Joshua, it is that he will need "Strength and Courage" for what is ahead. When God called him to lead Israel into the promise land, Moses had died and it was now his time to carry out the assignment given. It is not by coincidence that he is told to be strong and courageous because when something was really important throughout scripture it was always repeated. He is giving a set of instructions not only in how he is to lead the people but how he is to live his life before God and before the people.

As a leader you must keep in mind that when you are discouraged, the people following you will be as well. When you feel like giving up, the people who look up to you will also feel like giving up. So, pick your head up, straighten your back and walk in the power you have been given. You were born to lead; born to set the standard born to look the enemy in the face and not be moved. Your devotion to God and also the armor mentioned in our devotion yesterday are key elements to overcoming and winning every battle.

God desires your heart and also your mind to be in the right place. The more you feed yourself the word of God, the more it will become a part of your life. The world is looking for the secret to success, but you as a child of God, have access to unlock it daily by *Meditation.* That is right, the world is partially correct in their method of meditation. The problem is they are plugged into the wrong source! But you, you were born to lead, born to succeed through the word of God and the obedience of God's command.

Scripture Readings

Matthew 20: 26-28; Philippians 2:3-8

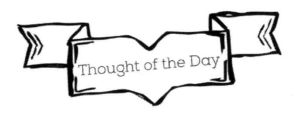

"You were born to lead; to teach; to raise the standard. This is what you were born for."

Questions: (for thought or discussion)

- What are the defining factors of a leader?
- Would you identify yourself as a leader or a follower? Why?
- Have you ever had a time in your life where you felt like the only way you succeeded was because of His strength? Explain the situation.
- Do you treat people according to Philippians 2:3, or do you often forget the worth and value that you are invest into others?
- What is your idea of success? How would you measure success?

Share with a friend what you did with God in place of the social media time.

Day 26

Pride comes before the Fall

---

*"After washing their feet, he put on his robe
again and sat down and asked, 'Do you
understand what I was doing? You call me
'Teacher' and 'Lord,' and you are right,
because that's what I am. And since I, your
Lord and Teacher, have washed your feet, you
ought to wash each other's feet. I have given
you an example to follow. Do as I have done to
you. I tell you the truth, slaves are not greater
than their master. Nor is the messenger more
important than the one who sends the
message. Now that you know these things, God
will bless you for doing them." John 13:12-17*

Jesus was the ultimate leader and yet He humbled
himself as a servant (Philippians 2:5-8). He showed and
prepared the way for his disciples, those who would lead
after his death. He set the example not only by what he said,
but also in his actions. The blessing Jesus speaks of in this
verse is not in what they know, but in how they applied what
he had taught them. For Jesus to wash the feet of his disciples
he was saying, "I am here for your sake. I am not hear of my
own benefit, but for the benefit of others." He looked for

nothing in return. How often are things done without expectation of repayment? It is rare. However, Jesus comes on the scene and makes it an everyday occurrence.

Do you understand that you relationship with Christ is an everyday encounter of grace and humility. Proverbs 16:18 says, "Pride goes before destruction, and haughtiness before a fall." It is important to stay grounded in the truth and in the "servant leadership" way of life. You are called and born to lead. But, you are also called to serve as you lead. Many times we think the two do not go together, but leadership and servant-hood go hand-in-hand. In order to lead you must be willing place the needs of others before your own.

You live a life every day that represents who God is to you and how you allow him to complete you. With him as your sustainer (he who provides and maintains) there is a responsibility you have to those who are following your lead. You must find a way to allow them to express their worth and value. The amazing thing about the leadership of Jesus, is all his disciples had a role. When you are leading your friends and helping them in their walk with God challenge them, helping them see they also have the ability and giftedness to lead. You have a responsibility to their personal growth with God. Challenge people around you to journal, have a consistent time for devotion, and spend time feeding themselves spiritually. As a leader, the example you set, is the example they will follow. Never think you are above the service of those who trust and look up to you. You need them just as much as they need you. As you lead others to Christ, you maintain your passion as well.

Scripture Readings

1 Corinthians 10:12; Romans 12:3; John 12:26

Thought of the Day

"As you live life as a leader, you also live life as a servant."

Questions: (for thought or discussion)

- In what ways do you feel your life is a service to God?
- Can you think of an opportunity you were given to serve? What was it? How did it make you feel?
- Challenge yourself to look for one person you can serve. Talk to someone about what you chose to do and what you thought about it.
- How is servant leadership carried out in your life? In what areas of your life do you display servant- leadership with friends, family or in school?

Today's Challenge

Write about how you felt on Day 24 when you turned off all communication.

Honor

"Children, obey your parents because you belong to the Lord, for this is the right thing to so. 'Honor your father and mother.' This is the first commandment with a promise: If you honor your father and mother, 'things will go well for, and you will have a long life on the earth." Ephesians 6:1-3

Honor is an interesting concept in the subject matter of parental relationships. Maybe you read this scripture over and over again and struggled to understand because your parents were not in your life or because you were abused. However, because God knows everything, he is also knew the hurt many would experience from a parent. But he also knew he would be a comforter and healer to the broken hearted.

If you are one who has had a rough relationship with a parent or maybe never met your biological parents, can I encourage you with this: In the depth of what you experienced and in the broken state of your heart, God desires to put those pieces back to together. Your honor for your father and mother is not based on if they were there or even if they were good parents, but honoring them because of the role they have in bringing you into this world.

When a person goes to court, they stand when the judge walks in. Do most people personally know the judge involved in their case, no. However, they stand because of the honor they have for the role. The fact that you honor your father and mother does not excuse the rough patches along the way. It does free you and place you in right standing with God because of your obedience to his decree. Also, your obedience to God's decree sets you up for a blessing because you chose to follow God's leading. You are blessed with long life as a result of it.

You may not always understand the decisions your parents make, but placing those doubts, worries, and fears in the hands of God is the best place for them. Honor is not something that is easily given, but when worth, value, and significance is understood, honor becomes natural and easier. Dig deep within and ask God to search your heart for possible areas where you have not forgiven. If you have a great relationship with your parents, take time out to tell them that you appreciate the sacrifices they made for you. They did not have to do it, but they did. Give honor where honor is due.

Scripture Readings

Colossians 3:20; Proverbs 23:22

Thought of the Day

"Honor your father and mother not because of what they have done but because of who

*they are. Who you are today is a result of your father and mother, who you will become is a result of you.***Questions: (for thought or discussion)**

- How often do you tell your parents you appreciate them?
- When did you feel the most loved by your parents?
- What is the greatest lesson you have learned from your parents?
- What do you hope to pass on to your children one day that you learned for your parents?

Today's Challenge

List three (3) of the most valuable lessons you have learned so far.

The way it used to be

"This what the Lord says: 'Stop at the crossroads and look around. Ask for the old, godly way, and walk in it. Travel its path, and you will find rest for your souls. But you reply, 'No, that's not the road we want!" Jeremiah 6:16

How often we forfeit peace because of our desire to be in control. Everyone wants to be the boss and no one wants to serve. How interesting it is that the Lord would give an opportunity for rest and peace and it be rejected. Can you imagine the blessings you could have had if you would have decided to sacrifice on school dance, sleep over, or basketball game. Often we miss out on what God is instructing because we do not want to listen.

Youth, how much more effective and influential could you be by taking the path that has been created by God, instead of taking matters into your own hands. Have you ever told your mom or dad that you were going one place, and ended up somewhere else? Has there ever been something bad that happens when you did that, but you are too ashamed to tell your parents because they were right about that group of friends? Chances are you could answer yes to most of the questions above. The reason behind the answer lies in control and pride.

When God, or even your parents, are trying to point you in the right direction it is not so you miss out on all of the "fun" stuff. It is so you are kept safe from all of the bad stuff. It is often hard to see the way things used to be because of the changes that have taken place today. But, as you allow God to lead your life as you lead others, make the decision at the crossroads to take the path less traveled. This path will lead to righteousness; this path will lead to trees that bear good fruit. Do not run into what you think is the right path, go to where you know God dwells.

Scripture Readings

Proverbs 14:12; Matthew 11:29, 7:13-14

"When you let go of you, you let in more of Him. The less of you, the more of Him."

Questions: (for thought or discussion)

- Can you recall a time where you felt so thankful you went back home when everyone was trying to convince you to go to the party and then you hear about what took place?
- Define the "path less traveled". What does look like to you as a youth?

- If a friend were to ask you why you make the decisions to stay away from negative environments, what would you say?
- How important do you think it is to stay on the path that God has instructed? What would say concerning taking the wrong path and the "grace factor"?

Ask your parents if there is something you could pray about for them.

Let it Go

"I don't mean to say that I have already achieved these things or that I have already reached perfection. But I press on to possess that perfection for which Christ Jesus first possessed me. No, dear brothers and sisters, I have not achieved it, but I focus on this one thing: Forgetting the past and looking forward to what lies ahead, I press on to reach the end of the race and receive the heavenly prize for which God, through Christ Jesus, is calling us."
Philippians 3:12-14

One of the greatest gifts you can give to yourself is the gift to "move on". I know they were your best friends and they turned on you. I know you were disappointed when you did not make the team, but be encouraged. Even though the things that happened did not feel good, you are still here. That is right. All of the things you had to let go of brought you closer to what God has for you. It may be hard to see while you are letting go and giving things up, but know that your gain is greater than what you gave.

God is not trying to keep things from you. He is trying to give you room to receive more of what He has for you. In order to be filled with more, you must also be empty. In order for God to make room for new opportunities, some will need to pass you by. In order to be who God has created you to be, you will need to let go of who you used to be.

To become more like Christ would mean to become less like you. The more your life is changed by the power of God, the more your light will shine. Do not allow the "give ups" to have you lose out on the gain. Even Paul understood his decisions to let go and see what he had received from God was a process. This does not happen overnight but it does happen to the extent you allow. You will see what you thought you wanted to do not and what you thought you needed, you can actually live without. You are in a race to win a prize that is eternal. A prize that is a mirror reflection of God's love and compassion.

Open your eyes to see the amazing privileges that come with knowing who your God is and what He has planned for your life.

Scripture Readings

Proverbs 3:5-6; Isaiah 43:18-19; Proverbs 4:25-27

"Letting go may not always be comfortable,
but letting go will always be worth it."

Questions: (for thought or discussion)

- Have you ever felt like you trusted your plan instead of trusting God's plan? What happened? Did you come to a point of letting go of your plan and welcoming God's plan?

- What does letting go look like for you? What are some things you had to let go of for God?
- Has God ever blessed you right after you made a sacrifice for him? In what way?
- Is there anything new that you see God doing in your life? If so, what?

Today's Challenge

Volunteer to do something at your youth group.

Run to Win

"Don't you realize that in a race everyone runs, but only one person gets the prize? So run to win! All athletes are disciplined in their training. They do it to win a prize that will fade away, but we do it for an eternal prize. So I run with purpose in every step. I am not just shadowboxing. I discipline my body like an athlete, training it to do what should. Otherwise, I fear that after preaching to others I myself might be disqualified." 1 Corinthians 9:24-27

Have you ever watched a race on television where the person who won actually started off losing? There is something that happens mid-way through the race where a sense of determination rises. The underdog comes out of nowhere, and blows the opponents out the water. At just the right time momentum is built and a speed that had not yet been displayed takes off. Often life creates a presence in the same way. You may start off feeling like you are losing in school, friendships, self-esteem, and the team you did not make. However, in the midst of what seemed to be a losing streak, a winner emerges.

You are that winner. You may not feel like it. You may not even look like it. You may even be losing at this very moment, but rest assured that there is a winner in you. There are people who are hoping and praying they will win the prize of "success" in this life. What God has designed for you is far much more than success in this life. You were born to win, so start running like you have already won the race. Pick yourself up from what the people in school said about you. Pick yourself up from what you did not have. Pick yourself up from what happened to you! You are a winner and no-matter what you have done or experienced, you can rise above it.

As your run in the race keep in mind you are running to win. You are not running in hopes of winning. You are running as a winner from the very beginning. It may not look like you are winning right now, but God has empowered you to finish strong and to finish with complete confidence in who you are. The prize awaiting you, is more beautiful and fulfilling than anything you could ever imagine. If you are going to run, Run to Win!

Scripture Readings

Isaiah 40:31; Hebrews 10:36

Thought of the Day

"It is not about how you start, it is about how you finish. Being that you started the race, you might as well win the race."

Questions: (for thought or discussion)

- Have you ever felt unmotivated to start a project but once you started, you actually enjoyed it? What does this tell you concerning how you start something?
- What does patient endurance mean to you? How do you maintain "patient endurance"?
- Name an area in your life where you could use some patient endurance?
- How can you maintain the "winner" mindset even when it looks like you are losing? How can you encourage others in this as well?

Do something that you've never done for God before, either publicly or privately.

Day 31

Speak life to Dry Bones

"The he asked me, 'Son of man, can these bones become living people again?' 'O, Sovereign Lord, 'I replied, 'you alone know the answer to that." Ezekiel 37:3

Have you ever been so tired either from homework, basketball practice, church, or chores you felt like you were going to literally pass out? Sure, you have. However, despite how you felt, somehow you mustered enough energy and strength to continue the day. You are not quite sure where the boost came from, but you are certain that just moments before you were completely drained. In a moment's time, God is able to restore strength and speak life. In a moments time God is able to use you to speak life to what looks dead.

In this scripture God gives instructions for words to be spoken over what appeared to be a valley of dry bones. A valley that lacked life and purpose. However, when the spoken word begins to be declared as instructed by God, something began to happen. Life was established with words, words demonstrated the power of God. In your life you will have situations that cause you to doubt and question if anything good can come from what you are experiencing. But, as you declare God's word with power, you will see change take place. You may not always understand what God is calling you to do, but keep in mind God does not require you to understand him, he asks only that you trust him.

Life and death are in the power of the tongue. Your ability to see beyond what your life or situation looks like will uplift and increase your faith. If you place your life or your situation that looks dead (grades, relationship, home life, finances) in the hands of God, He can breathe the breath of life into it. It is true that only God knows what will be, but it is also true that according to your faith, so shall it be given unto you. What are you willing to trust God with? Are you willing to place the most challenging situation at the feet of Jesus or only the easy problems you are not afraid to give to him? If you allow God to empower you, to speak life for yourself and to yourself, you allow Him to empower you for others. You will see in your scripture reading how what God instructs Ezekiel to do was not just for his faith to be activated, but also for the people who would receive a prophetic word (Spirit led truth, instruction, future declaration) of God's provision.

Keep this in mind, your ability to trust God and to speak life over things and people who have been counted out is not only for your faith to be established. This is also so others might believe as well. Dare to trust him. Dare to speak life.

Scripture Reading
Ezekiel 37:1-14

Thought of the Day

"Speaking life to what appears dead activates your faith to a level of miraculous encounters. Your ability to trust the instructions of God in what looks impossible creates a life that sees no limit."

Questions: (for thought or discussion)

- Has God ever used you to help someone see that there is life after what they have experienced? How so?
- Can you recall a time where you thought life was so bad that there was no way things would change and God turned it around by using you to speak life?
- How does it make you feel to know there will be situations in your life that appear dead? Hopeless? Do you feel powerful in knowing God has given you the ability to speak life? Or, are you afraid you will not have enough faith to believe?
- Is there anything going on in your life right now that you can speak life to? What can you do in this moment to see the situation God's way?

Today's Challenge

Pay for a stranger's meal and leave a note,
"God loves to surprise us, He loves You."

Ask for it

---

*"I will give you what you asked for! I will give a
wise and understanding heart such as no one
else has had or ever will have! And I will also
give you what you did not ask for- riches and
fame! No other king in all the world will be
compared to you for the rest of your life! And if
you follow me and obey my decrees and my
commands as your father, David, did, I will
give you a long life."1 Kings 3:12-13*

Solomon could have asked for anything in the world.
Fame, fortune, security, and the list goes on. However, he
asked for what would benefit not only him, but more
importantly, the people he had been called to lead. Can you
imagine what you would have asked for if you knew there
were no limits to what God would give? The list goes from
one extreme to the other. You are probably traveling down
"wonderland" as you think of all the things you desire at this
very moment. Maybe you have a desire to be a movie star, a
professional athlete, a missionary in Uganda or a doctor.
Maybe your dreams are full of ambition and heart for others.
Whatever those dreams and desires may be, challenge
yourself in considering that God promises he will not

withhold any good thing from you (Psalm 84:11) as you walk uprightly before him.

There are no limits to what God can do as you live your life daily for Him. Challenge yourself to think out-of-the-box from what society has created as great attainment. Begin to think of what you could or who you could become that would bring people to know Christ as Lord and Savior. While, there is nothing wrong with desiring things in this world, keep in mind that even though you are in this world, you are not of it. Ultimately only what you do and strive towards brings glory to God, and brings satisfaction to you. Solomon understood he had been placed as a leader over people. He knew He would need wisdom above and beyond anything He could attain on his own. Allow yourself to be challenged today to think above and beyond the norm.

Look at how God blessed Solomon. Not only does He give him what he asked for, he also gave him what he did not ask for, all because his heart was in the right place. At the end of the day, look at all you already have and consider all you lack. What could you use right now the most that would not only empower you but empower others? The blessings God desires to give you will exceed anything you could imagine, so do not settle when God desires to have your cup run over. Ask God to search your heart daily, allowing you to see what is there, that may be motivated by self gain. Ask him to open your eyes to see that what you lack, you can ask for and what you need, you can ask for as well. There is no lack in the storehouse of God. According to His will, so shall it be given. Ask for it!

Scripture Readings

1 Kings 3:1-14; Ephesians 3:20; John 16:24; Psalm 91:16; Philippians 4:19

"God desires to surprise you. Do not allow your thinking to become limited to what everyone else is receiving."

Questions: (for thought or discussion)

- If you could ask God for anything, what would it be and why?
- How would you define long life? Would you relate that to a specific age or level of fulfillment in life?
- How does it make you feel to know God desires to bless you and to give you things? Can you imagine a gift that not only benefits you, but others around you? What would the gift be?
- Do you feel like your needs are being supplied as in Philippians 4:19? What would you identify as "needs" and are there people currently living in the world without those "needs?" If so, what does that mean to you?

Share the Live Out Loud Pledge with a friend.

Living a Life of Freedom and Truth

---

*"Jesus said to the people who believed in him,
'You are truly my disciples if you remain
faithful to my teachings. And you will know
the truth, and the truth will set you free.' 'But
we are descendants of Abraham,' they said.
'We have never been slaves to anyone. What do
you mean, 'You will be set free'?' Jesus replied,
'I tell you the truth, everyone who sins is a
slave of sin. A slave is not a permanent member
of the family, but a son is part of the family
forever. So if the Son sets you free, you are
truly free." John 8:31-36*

Freedom is a choice we decide upon daily. In the decision of choosing freedom, the decision to also choose truth is just as important. In fact, the two work together as a team. Have you ever met a person who you could not trust, and as a result of this the friendship was limited? It is a direct indicator that in order to love freely, in order to become vulnerable and in order to establish something of great worth, truth must be present. Jesus spoke to his disciples telling them their relationship with him was built upon their level of faithfulness to his teachings. In this same way, your relationship with God is built upon consistency and continual commitment that is lived out daily.

The world is searching for truth and for something to hold on to. Temptation becomes appealing when your desire and interest for God decreases. This happens in various ways. It could take the form of peer pressure, media influence, family issues, self-esteem, or something not as obvious. If your passion for God decreases, an opportunity is available for the world to try and fill God's place in your heart. This is why you must guard your hear; your mind must be focused; and the company you keep must reflect where you desire to be with God. Jesus made it clear to his disciples that once you are freed through Christ, you are free indeed. However, allowing your life to be surrendered to God's plan is a daily decision and daily choice.

It is important to understand how your freedom empowers you to do and what God has created you to do. At time you may struggle with living a dedicated life to God but as you surrender your all to God, you allow yourself to be clothed in truth. That place of truth and freedom is the same place where you will shine in the midst of darkness. You have been made free and complete because of Christ and that freedom is ever lasting. Are you willing to reflect your love and commitment to God out of the obedience of His word? Are you willing to live a life of freedom, as you live a life of truth even when friends do not agree?

Scripture Readings

John 16:13, 4:24, 1:14; Psalm 25:5

Thought of the Day

*"Your passion towards freedom in Christ
will always lead you to truth."*

Questions: (for thought or discussion)

- When was the last time your relationship with God influenced your decision to be honest with a friend? What have you done or said lately that was done in truth because of your desire to represent God?
- How does it make you feel to know your freedom is based on your faithfulness to God? If your freedom is established by your surrender to God, how could you live a life of freedom daily?
- How can you represent Christ to your friends who do not know him, while demonstrating the importance of being honest even in situations that may make you feel uncomfortable?

Today's Challenge

Give someone a Bible.

Day 34

It's your Choice

"But if you refuse to serve the Lord, then choose today whom you will serve. Would you prefer the gods of your ancestors served beyond the Euphrates? Or will it be the gods of the Amorites in whose land you now live? But as for me and my family, we will serve the Lord." Joshua 24:15

Each and every day the enemy seeks to steal your attention from God. He desires for you to chase the artificial and temporary "gain" of the world. However, you must be bold and strong in what God has called you to and who God has called you to be. You have been created with purpose to be an example for those who are lost, feeling forgotten, depressed, and alone. In order to be the light and example you must daily choose to surrender and serve only God.

There will be moments, even days when what the world advertises catches your eye, but keep in mind that only what you do for God will last. What you gain in the world can be lost in a moment. While, what you gain in Christ is a lifelong and eternal guarantee. Joshua was giving instructions leaving the people with one of two choices: serve God or not. There was no in-between. There was no concept of "think about it and come to a conclusion tomorrow." The decisions needed to be made, and delay was not an option. In life you will be challenged with what your friends claim are cool things to partake in. You will even have days where you feel like you are missing out on what is deemed "fun." But, be encouraged that there is no limit to the blessings God has in store for those who remain faithful.

God desires to bless you in a way so other people see God in you. So people will look at you and desire the same God you are serving. One of amazing benefits of about being a partner with Christ in God's Kingdom, is you get the opportunity to help build the Kingdom and see the great things taking place in the lives of your peers. You do not have to be afraid because God is with you. He will surround you with people who love Him and have a desire to show God's love and to live out that love as well. Keep in mind that your choice, is just that "yours". God will not force you, He desires for you to want him above all else. Will you choose Him above all, not just on Sundays or at your youth group but every day, surrendering to his will for your life?

Scripture Readings

1 Peter 2:9; Mark 8:36; Proverbs 22:1

*"Who you choose today will be who you live
for tomorrow. So choose wisely."*

Questions: (for thought or discussion)

- In what ways has God called you out of darkness as descried in 1 Peter 2:9?
- What things could you do on a daily basis to remind yourself of the worth and value you have in serving God?
- How can you help others see the joy and delight in placing God first?
- What are some blessings you have seen God give as a result of you making a daily decision to choose him?
- How has God revealed your worth to you as it relates to being a child of the King?
- Think of things that have happened in your life that you know God was protecting you from, even when all of your friends were doing it. How does it make you feel to look back and see that God was not trying to keep things from you, he was trying to protect you from the things that would keep you from him?

Today's Challenge

Share your testimony with some friends or with someone who feels alone.

Day 35

Seek Him First

*"Seek the Kingdom of God above all else, and
live righteously, and he will give you
everything you need." Matthew 6:33*

Have you ever thought of what life would be like without God? Have you ever thought about all you would miss out on without having God in your life as King? These are big questions, for sure. However, the bigger question is "How much of your life do you really feel God deserves?" Now, that is a tough one, so think on it for a minute or two. Ultimately, the worth and value you place on God will be the same level of worth in your life that you are willing to give to Him. Above all, He loves you. You come second to none and throughout scriptures he speaks highly of your value (Psalm 139:16-18). He desires to have all of you and as a result of giving all of yourself, you give God room to bless above and beyond what you could imagine.

Matthew said that as followers of Christ and as God's mouthpieces in a world that has gone silent, we are to place His Kingdom above all else. Now, you may be thinking you do not have a Kingdom to place above God's. However, think again, because anything you desire or long after has the possibility of taking God's place in your heart. Of becoming an idol, or potentially your own Kingdom. You see a kingdom is any place of value that has been built out of self-gain and not Holy Spirit inspired. What Matthew is demonstrating in this scripture is being able to trust God enough to take care of His work before being concerned with our own. This requires you to see the bigger picture God has in mind for you.

As you take care of God's Kingdom, God takes care of your desires, dreams, and goals. More than you want to see those dreams of yours comes to past, God does even the more. He knows when you have shown yourself faithful and trustworthy to receive what you have asked for. Make God your priority. Allow God to be your first love and the motivation behind everything you do. Following that path, will lead you to joy and fulfillment because the path you have chosen has been created as a result of seeking God above all things. Trust He will not lead you astray. Trust with all your heart just as you daily choose to seek God's Kingdom above all, God continually blesses you above and beyond what you could do for yourself as well.

Scripture Readings

Matthew 22:37, 6:24; Luke 2:49, 6:38

"In order for God to fill you with more, you must first be willing to pour all that you have out. It requires no faith to maintain

*what you have. However, it does require
faith to believe God for what you do not
have."*

Questions: (for thought or discussion)

- How can you seek God's Kingdom first as a youth?
- What are some of the main distractions that try to keep you from seeking God first?
- Can you recall a time where you did not seek God first and did what you wanted, only to realize you missed something amazing God had for you? How did you feel? What was your response?
- Have there been some occurrences in your life where you gave something to God and He blessed you with more than what you gave up?
- If so, how can those experiences help you in relating to your friends in God not wanting to take away you fun, but give you a life that is more fun in Him, than without him?

*Extend the opportunity of salvation to a
friend.*

Day 36

Do what is right

"You say, 'I am allowed to do anything'- but not everything is good, for you. You say, 'I am allowed to do anything' - but not everything is beneficial. Don't be concerned for your own good but for the good of others."
1 Corinthians 10:23-24

You are privileged beyond belief as a child of the King. There are in fact no limits outside of what you create. You serve an amazing, limitless God. However, God gives freedom to choose his will or to give in to our own. The decision we make has the ability to either limit us or free us. This may be hard at times; this may even challenge you to refrain from doing certain things for the sake of helping others. Paul states you have been given freedom and the free will to choose what you will do. But, that choice comes with a price that can either benefit you and others around you or will be a stumbling block for those who are looking to you as leader.

At this point, you have spent almost 40 days diving into God's word. Allowing yourself to be challenged and removing the limitations from your thinking. Your eyes have been opened to all God has made available. Your ability to receive what God has is found in your ability to remain faithful and true to God's word and to your convictions as well. Sometimes decisions are made out of pressure and in those times, when the struggle is real, you can ask God to give you strength and to present a way of escape for you. There will be situations that come up causing you to feel like the "odd ball" out. However, when it is all done, those people are the same ones who will respect and appreciate you.

People may not always say you have inspired them or that you have given them hope but you can be confident of this, "They are watching you". Your freedom will be the open door to your friends and to those who are family as well. Remain strong in all God is leading you to do and know there is a due season for everything. A season where you will reap all God has for you, if you do not give up (Galatians 6:9). You may feel like giving up. You may even feel like all you have done just isn't worth the sacrifice, but you can be honest with God concerning how you feel. You can place every worry and doubt at his feet. In this, you place the control in God's hands. You place the deciding factor in God's hand. You allow God to be the leader of your heart and the leader of your decisions. As a result of you allowing God to lead you, you then have a mindset that is set out to do what is right, even if it is not comfortable.

Scripture Readings

Judges 21:25; Isaiah 1:17; Deuteronomy 6:18

Thought of the Day

"Doing what is right may not be the popular thing to do, but it will always be the positive thing to do."

Questions: (for thought or discussion)

- Do you feel doing what is right becomes easier as you grow with God? Have you seen that happen in your life?
- How do you feel about living your life so others do not stumble?
- How can you develop more confidence in what you believe even when your friends do not agree?
- In what ways can you apply Isaiah 1:17 to your life daily?
- Can you recall a time where you made the right decision and your friends came to you later, saying they wish they would have followed your lead? If so, how did that make you feel?
- How can you relate to Judges 21:25?

Today's Challenge

Ask God to show you who He wants you to pray for. Go into a public place with the intention of praying for someone and follow through with it.

A Clean Heart

"Create in me a clean heart, O God. Renew a loyal spirit within me." Psalm 51:10

You are closer than you think to the life you have always wanted. You have searched for acceptance and genuine friendship and that is what God desires to give you. He desires for you to live each day feeling accepted and loved in a way like never before. This love and acceptance will not be found on your sports team, your class, and or even with your best friend. This love and acceptance is found in a relationship with God. Daily, God longs for you to have a heart open to change and open to receive all that is of Him.

As you live your life daily as a billboard for Christ, people will wonder what makes you so different. You will be living proof that there are no limits to what God can do Living proof of what God has done. One of the key factors in maintaining open and consistent communication is allowing God to do a work in your heart. Ask him to create in you a clean heart, not just once, but daily. The enemy desires to get your attention and he will stop at nothing to try and distract from your love for God. However, as God continually transforms your life by the renewing of your mind, the enemy loses the battle every time.

As you grow continually with each new day, you are challenged to take all you have learned and use it to help and bless your friends. There may be people who have been hurt or betrayed by friends or even family and they need God to create a clean heart within them. Your personal experiences will help them through what they are facing. The fact you have welcomed God into your heart and you give Him permission to clean up and clean out everything that does not look like him is proof God loves you right where you are. But, it is also proof he loves you so much not to leave you where you are.

The love God has for you and the plan God has for is not based on anything you have done or anything you could ever earn. His love for you goes to the deepest depth and nothing can separate you from his love. In a silent world you have been called to live out loud, may friends, neighbors and even strangers see that your life is a light everywhere that you go.

Scripture Readings

1 Samuel 16:7; Psalm 26:2; Proverbs 4:23

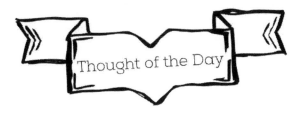

Thought of the Day

"May God be the treasure of your heart not only with words but in action."

Questions: (for thought or discussion)

- What does guarding your heart mean to you in reference to Proverbs 4:23? What are practical ways that you can do this?
- Can you think of a time where God revealed to you something in your heart that was not of him? How were you changed?
- How does it make you feel to know that even though God knows every secret and everything that has ever entered your heart He still loves you?
- What can you do daily to make sure your heart is in the right place? Create a list of five (5) practical steps that can help you in this process.

Today's Challenge

Share something on social media that has been a challenge to overcome and how God has helped you through.

Day 38

Return

---

*"He looked at them and said, 'Go show
yourselves to the priests.' And as they went,
they were cleansed of their leprosy. One of
them, when he saw that he was healed, came
back to Jesus, shouting, 'Praise God!' He fell to
the ground at Jesus' feet, thanking him for
what he had done. This man was a Samaritan.
Jesus asked, 'Didn't I heal ten men? Where are
the other nine? Has no one returned to give
glory to God except the foreigner?' And Jesus
said to the man, 'Stand up and go. Your faith
has healed you."* Luke 17:14-19

Jesus lived a public life of healing, freedom, and
deliverance. People knew who he was because his presence
went before him. His life was one of influence and great
authority. People would meet Jesus and immediately
received healing. However, just like our society today, we get
so caught up in the gift (healing, blessings, etc) that
sometimes we forget or fail to return and express gratitude.
There is so much to be thankful for and each day you wake
up is one more reason to lift your hands to God and say,
"Thank You".

One can only imagine how Jesus must have felt when only one came back to say thank you. How have you felt in the past where your gift, love, or presence was not appreciated? I imagine, not good. What led the one man to return? Could it have been he thought to himself of how he felt when gratitude was not expressed? Could it have been the fact he was completely overwhelmed and shocked by what had taken place? It could have been a mixture of both or maybe neither, but what we do know is he came back.

The better question may be, what kept the other lepers from returning to say, "Thank You"? Maybe in their own way, they were carrying out what was asked of them. After all, Jesus did say, "Go show yourselves to the priest". Sometimes, God gives us room to decide whether we follow just what is asked or if we will search possibilities of giving God more. The nine lepers did not sin in not returning, they did what was asked. However, there is something to be said for the person who goes above what is expected and searches for other ways to give back more. Challenge yourself to not settle with just doing what is asked, go above and beyond. God blessed Solomon with what he asked for, but he also went above and beyond that as well. It is okay to do more. In fact, you are welcomed to exhaust opportunities where you may be a blessing.

Can you imagine being blessed above and beyond anything you could imagine by someone and never saying, "Thank You"? Your ability to express a grateful heart is your ability to recognize and acknowledge a level of kindness and generosity that did not have to be displayed. In society, the notion or perception of "entitlement" is a huge problem. Ultimately, everything given to us is by the grace of God. There is nothing that could be said or done to deserve or earn the amazing love God has for his children. During this season of your life, allow yourself to see back, reflect on all

God has done. You may not have everything you want, but at this very moment the fact that you are alive proves you have everything you need in order to live. Take time, and return to the Father, thanking Him for all that He has done, is doing, and will do. Your life is a blessing so you might be a blessing to others. Do not forget to return.

Scripture Readings

1 John 4:10; Psalm 100:4; 2Corinthians 2:14; Philippians 4:6

Thought of the Day

"Having a heart of gratitude positions you for overflow. Having a heart of entitlement closes the door of blessings."

Questions: (for thought or discussion)

- What are ways you can express your appreciation to God for all the things He has done?
- How do you feel, knowing God loved you first and that you have done nothing to earn that love?
- Do you feel there have been times in your life when you have been like the nine who did not return to say, "Thank You?" If so, how or why?
- What are you the most thankful for? How have you returned to God in expressing your gratitude for that specific thing?

- How would you help your friends or illustrate for your friends what a life of "returning" looks like?

Conduct a Bible Study with friends in a public place.

From Darkness to Light

"But you are not like that, for you are a chosen people. You are royal priests, a holy nation, God's very own possession. As a result, you can show others the goodness of God, for he called you out of the darkness into his wonderful light". 1 Peter 2:9

You are God's chosen generation. Your life story (your testimony) is a reflection of what God has brought you from, but it is also a reflection of where he is taking you. You have desired more of God and as a result God will fill you. In living your life as a billboard for all to see, keep in mind that your life is a "lighthouse" for many of your friends. You are a place of safety. You have been called out of the life you used to live and into a new life with Christ. Above all God desires for your relationship with Him to be intimate and consistent. In the natural, when you like someone, you spend time with them. Well, with God it is even the more important to spend time in His presence.

According to 1 Peter, God has not called you out just to call you out! No, God has called you out to bring you into something amazing and beautiful. A life that is able to speak out, live out, and stand out. When you live your life this way, others are able to identify with you and see one of their peer's sell out for God. Make it your daily routine to lay your life down for God. Place your ideas at God's feet and allow him to be your everything. Allow God to blow you away with endless possibilities as you acknowledge the limitations you have without him.

You have been called out of darkness and many of your friends will not understand. Some of your friends will say that ever since you started the 40 day journey with God, you changed. But, it is okay because they are right. When you let God change your mind, and you are willing to embrace who He is in you, life certainly changes. You will be challenged and often you may even feel like you have to prove yourself, but you do not. Remember, your life is a billboard of what people see, of what you reflect in your day to day life. Life will look different and you will notice how you have changed, but also how some around you have not. Just as Solomon asked for wisdom, you should do the same.

God loves you and though this 40 day devotional is coming to an end, know that your journey with the King is just beginning. Living out Loud in a Silent world will now be the fabric of your life, the pep in your step, and the rhythm of your life. Your anchor is in God's truth and He will not lead you astray.

Scripture Readings

2 Corinthians 6:14-18; John 8:12; 3:18-21, 1 John 1:5-7

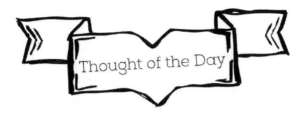

*"You are the light the world is looking for,
do not hide it. The light who is Christ,
desires to shine through you."*

Questions: (for thought or discussion)

- What does being called out of the darkness mean to you?
- Are there any moments when people look to you to be the light? If so, how?
- Do you feel confident to be the light your friends are looking for? How do you maintain that light in darkness?
- What are tools or steps you could use daily in being a light in your school and also within your family?
- How bright is your light? Check your light daily.

*Invite a group of friends over to your house
to pray for any needs they may have.*

Live Out Loud

"For I am not ashamed of this Good News about Christ. It is the power of God at work, saving everyone who believes- the Jew first and also the Gentile. This Good News tells us how God makes us right in his sight. This is accomplished from start to finish by faith. As the Scriptures say, "It is through faith that a righteous person has life". Romans 1:16 -17

Living out Loud in a Silent World is understanding who you are and more importantly whose you are. If you know your creator, you then have access to the purpose behind the creation. The reason why you may feel at times like you are lost is because of a lack of relationship with the Creator. If you try to figure out what the Creator had in mind for his creation (you) without knowing His heart, you will face rough times. The world is living out loud, but saying "nothing," no true purpose, while often times the children of God who are the mouthpiece of God remain quiet.

Your friends do not ignore God because they do not want Him. They ignore God because they do not know Him. However, you have been called to be that billboard to introduce them to God as they meet you. Your life should be a living and walking example of who God is and the love God has. Some of your friends have rejected the truth of God because of seeing people act one way in church and another way outside of church, but you have been called out to be different. Take pride and great responsibility for living your life daily as God desires. Do not allow the thoughts of others to stop your expression of God as King in your life.

Youth all over this world are taking a stand for freedom in Christ, will you? Will you allow your life to shine, never being shamed of Jesus Christ because it is truth? You have been on a journey for 40 days with God. Throughout this time change has been taking place in your life. People are noticing something different in you. Do not ignore that. Challenge yourself to want more, to be more, and to live out loud. Sure, there will be people who do not agree, but that is okay. Your job is not to convince people. Your job is to allow the love of God to shine through you, so others might see Him.

According to 1 John 4:7-19, as you live in God, your love grows more perfectly. This is what you have been called to. Live out Loud with God, Live out Loud with Love. Do not spend another day holding back or feeling awkward. God has given you strength and courage to be a leader and to stand on God's word. This is your time to stand up and to live out loud! Your journey is only beginning.

Scripture Readings

1 Timothy 4:7-10; Hebrews 10:36; 1 Peter 4:1-6

Thought of the Day

"Living out Loud in a Silent World is walking out your faith in every step. Letting God lead you in what you do and say on a daily basis. Do not glide through your faith, walk it out."

Questions: (for thought or discussion)

- What does living out loud mean to you?
- What are the main challenges that you have faced in living out loud?
- How can you conquer those challenges?
- In what ways can you demonstrate this life around people who do not know God?
- What is your motivation for living out loud?
- What would be the best way for you to live out loud?

Today's Challenge

Give this devotional to a friend and recommend it to others.

"Live Out Loud" Pledge

I pledge to live a life that is committed to God in every way. My love for God will not be altered because of the thoughts and opinions of others.

I was born to stand out so I refuse to fit in. It is my desire to be an example of what a "Sold Out" life looks like and I will not bend my personal convictions to fit it.

I will not compromise my relationship with God to establish superficial friendships, relationships or status.

I believe God gave His one and only Son, Jesus Christ as described in John 3:16 for my sins and that I might live an abundant life with Christ.

I believe my life is a reflection of God's amazing love and Jesus laying his life down for me.

I am thankful that in the same way Jesus was raised from the dead, my old life has also been buried and raised in him.

I have a new life today because of what Jesus did for me. I am devoted to God and I turn my back to this world, vowing to live a life out loud in a world that is silent.

PRAYER POSTURE

(Complete Discipleship Curriculum available at miraclereed.com)

The most important factor in any relationship is communication. This is the same with your relationship with the Lord. You must be willing to "still" yourself in order to hear the voice of God. It is in the silence that He speaks!

"Be still, and know that I am God." Psalm 46:10

Exercise: What do you see when you look at yourself? Take a moment a jot down your first thoughts and feelings. This is not only an indicator of self-perception, but also your connection with God's view of you! Be Transparent, Be Real, Be Free!

I. **Allow God to be God**
   A. In order to recognize the worth and value that lives on the inside of you, God must first be properly positioned in your life. This requires sacrifice and humility.
   B. Keep in mind the "Thin Line between humility and condemnation" and how that translates in your relationship and understanding of God.
   C. Read Jeremiah 29:13

II. **How does He Speak**
   A. I Kings 19- Stillness
   B. John 14:6- Leaves no other option
   C. Genesis 1,2,3- Power, Life, Certainty

III. Properly Positioned (PRAYER POSTURE)
A. Sit- Comfortable (Don't Rush)
B. Still- Remove Yourself from Distractions/Clear Mind
C. Wait- Just Listen

This may seem like a bit of a challenge. Over a period of time this will become your "prayer posture". There is nothing like spending time with God and hearing Him speak. He does so in various ways and is not boxed into to a specific way. It may be audible, visual, thought, sound, feeling, etc.

Tools to use when you feel like Being Silent

1. Spend some time in prayer with God and include "Prayer Posture."

2. Remind yourself that your life is a billboard. Every day you have the ability to either speak life or death, not only with your words, but in your actions as well.

3. Remind yourself that you have been called out to be a leader. The plan God has for you has no "clock out" time.

4. Remind yourself of where you came from and where God has taken you.

5. Remind yourself of all the people who have been led to God because of your "Yes."

6. Ask someone what they see in you since you began your 40 day journey.

7. Review your response to the questions throughout your 40 day devotional.

8. Take a moment and think of how much it cost for you to have the joy and freedom that you now experience in your life, something you never had before.

9. Remind yourself that in your weakness God's strength is made perfect. God welcomes you with open arms even when you feel like giving up. Your weakness does not disqualify you.

10. Lastly, tell yourself, "I have not done all that I have done, given all that I gave, and surrendered my life to Christ with everything within me, to allow the world to shut me up. I will not keep silent. My life will speak volumes."

The Author

Connect with Miracle:

Social Media

- Facebook.com/miracle.reed/
- Twitter @MiracleReed
- Instagram: Iammissmiracle

**For more information or booking visit
www.miraclereed.com**

Miracle Reed is a native of Pittsburgh, Pennsylvania and has been committed to serving God since 1996. It was certainly apparent from the very beginning that her life would be an inspiration to many. She was born three months premature, weighing 1.6 pounds at birth, placing her in the twentieth percentile of babies who survive weighing a little over a pound. Not only did the Great Physician take over, but He also allowed the life of one to prove to all those who would meet her that nothing is impossible with God. It is no wonder why her name is Miracle!

Miracle being the daughter of parents that have struggled with drug addiction, gives her a platform and relativity to stand tall as an Advocate of Hope and Inspiration for people who have been challenged with this same storm. She provides and presents "The way" for people, in seeing first hand a process of freedom within the lives of her own parents. People often wonder, "How she managed to accomplish all that she has, with experiencing great turmoil, neglect, and confusion." She often responds with, "I knew from the time I was a child that I could either feel alone, live in sorrow and anger or I could become empowered by every experience, building a *Bridge of Hope* for others, while creating one for myself. I chose the latter." Her obedience, passion and love for God have given her the opportunities to not only preach, but counsel and pastor not only in the United States, but the Caribbean and now Canada; where she currently lives.

Miracle believes the only limit in life is that which we create. We must become open to God without restraints to truly live without limits. She is living proof of how there are no limits when God is in control. It is her desire to live a life inspiring others to welcome the *plan of God and experience the beauty of a life devoted to Him.*

Miracle is a graduate of the Marilyn J. Davis School of the Bible, where she received her license for ministry as well as a diploma in the Bible. She also graduated of Geneva College, where she received bachelor's degrees in both Biblical Studies and Human Services. She has created ministry discipleship programs and workshops designed to bring forth healing, complete wholeness, family restoration, and inspiration. She is the author of *When God Vetoes Your Plan* and creator of the *Why Me/Yes You* discipleship course. Miracle loves God and has a passion to fulfill His plan above all things. She lives each day humbled by the opportunities of being a part of that plan. She is currently the Associate Pastor of Timbers Community Church in British Columbia, Canada, which is nothing short of an act of God. Truly, God has been faithful and out of the box, as He continues to send her to various places in the world.